THE POWER OF KARMA YOGA

THE POWER OF KARMA YOGA

Decoding Ancient Wisdom for Lasting Success

GOPINATH CHANDRA DAS

JAICO PUBLISHING HOUSE

Ahmedabad Bangalore Chennai
Delhi Hyderabad Kolkata Mumbai

Published by Jaico Publishing House
A-2 Jash Chambers, 7-A Sir Phirozshah Mehta Road
Fort, Mumbai - 400 001
jaicopub@jaicobooks.com
www.jaicobooks.com

© Gopinath Chandra Das

THE POWER OF KARMA YOGA
ISBN 978-81-19153-99-2

First Jaico Impression: 2023
Second Jaico Impression: 2023

No part of this book may be reproduced or utilized in
any form or by any means, electronic or
mechanical including photocopying, recording or by any
information storage and retrieval system,
without permission in writing from the publishers.

Page design and layout by Jojy Philip, Delhi

Printed by
Trinity Academy For Corporate Training Limited, Mumbai

CONTENTS

Introduction: Our Egos, Our Identities, and Our Struggles to Let Go   1

PART I
The Subtle Art of Letting Go

1. The Art of Letting Go – I: Through Saankhya   19
2. The Art of Letting Go – II: Through Yoga   30
3. Making Letting Go a Lesser Ordeal: By Adhering to Aparigraha   40

PART II
Going from Want-Driven to Purpose-Driven

4. The Want-Driven and the Purpose-Driven: A Comparison   51
5. Evolving from Being Want-Driven to Being Purpose-Driven: Through Yajnas   60
6. Hurdles on the Way to a Purpose-Driven Life: Controllership and Doership   68

7. Unleashing the Power of Dependency:
Through Rituals   76

8. Relying on Trust Is Unavoidable: Whether in
Material Life or Spiritual Life   82

9. The Purpose-Driven Vis-à-Vis the Responsibility-
Driven: Their Similarities and Differences   90

PART III
In Search of a Worthy Purpose

10. Being Purpose-Driven: What Does
It Really Mean?: A Deeper Look   101

11. Finding Reciprocation for Being Purpose-Driven:
Do You Feel That You Are Appreciated and Your
Love Is Requited?   109

12. Investing Yourself in More than One Purpose:
Is That a Better Option?   119

13. Is Your Purpose-Driven Life on a Slippery Slope?:
The Dangers of Not Finding a Worthy Purpose   126

14. The Purpose That Drives a Karma Yogi:
Transcendental Service   132

PART IV
Advancing in Karma Yoga

15. Harness the Power of Simplicity: Its Five Benefits   141

16. Tap the Power of Your Intelligence:
Analysing Intelligence   153

CONTENTS

17. Tap the Guru's Wisdom: Through Submission, Inquiry, and Service — 161

18. Reaching the Summit of Karma Yoga: The Awakening of Jnana — 177

PART V
The Perfection of Karma Yoga

19. The Life of a Karma Yogi: An Example from Modern Times — 187

20. Experiencing the Divine in Karma Yoga: Through Sankirtana Yajna — 200

INTRODUCTION
Our Egos, Our Identities, and Our Struggles to Let Go

March 27, 1964. "37 Who Saw Murder Didn't Call the Police" was a front-page splash in *The New York Times*. While the headline declared there were 37 bystanders, the article said there were 38. The write-up described how for more than half an hour "respectable, law-abiding citizens in Queens watched a killer stalk and stab" 28-year-old Kitty Genovese. "I didn't want to get involved," one onlooker had admitted to the police during the investigation.

The article gained much traction, and the episode became the emblem of urban apathy in America. It triggered academic studies, and the incident eventually made its way into psychology textbooks, which called this tendency of witnesses to distance themselves from a crime scene the "bystander effect," or the "Kitty Genovese syndrome."

On the personal front, Kitty's brother, 16-year-old Bill Genovese, was among the most affected.

When he was 19, Bill readily enlisted in the Marines to fight in the Vietnam War. While his friends saw America's intervention in Vietnam as tragic and schemed to dodge the draft, for him that kind of evasion smacked of the same apathy that shadowed his sister's murder. In an interview with *The Washington Post,* Bill said he had responded to America's call to arms because he "didn't want to be like the 38 witnesses."

Bill was injured on the war front in Vietnam and lost both his legs.

Calling Bill an egomaniac would sound way off the track and downright absurd. But was it his ego that pushed him—covertly—into a war that left him physically challenged?

For an answer, we need to better understand the ego's working.

The Ego

For starters, let's discuss the positive indispensable role that the ego plays in our lives—as paradoxical as that may sound!

The ego—*ahankara* in Sanskrit—gives us our identities. Under the ego's influence, I see myself as an Indian, a monk, a disciple, a son, and so on. And once I know who I am, I also know what I should be doing. Put differently, our identities define our thoughts, words, and actions. As an Indian, I am patriotic, seek opportunities to glorify our country's ancient culture and teachings, and behave as a responsible citizen. As a monk, I think spiritually, try to avoid mundane gossip, and strive to serve society selflessly. As a disciple, my thoughts are disciplined and so are my words and actions. As a son, I desire good health for my ageing parents, call them up regularly, and visit them once in a while. Waking up every morning, I don't find myself in limbo, endlessly wondering how I should spend the day. My identities bring to mind my responsibilities—and I am out and about. Put differently, the ego's job is to ensure we know who we are and behave accordingly.

The ego gets toxic, however, when it endlessly defends identities that it has given. Take, for example, the story of the American inventor Edwin Land.

Edwin Land, best known for co-founding Polaroid Corporation, invented the instant camera in 1948, following which his company took off. For three decades Polaroid ruled the world of photography. In 1980, Sony founder Akio Morita confided in Land that the camera niche seemed to be on the cusp of digitalisation; he expressed interest in collaborating on an electronic camera. The idea was lost on Land, who reasoned that customers would always want a print, and the quality of digital images could never match that of chemically processed ones.

As it turned out, Land was wrong. But absurdly, even as Polaroid Corporation suffered in the emerging digital market, Land was unwilling to come around. He shielded himself with devout followers who supported his adamancy to continue pouring the company's resources into traditional non-digital research. Eventually, the mounting losses forced the Polaroid board to oust Land from the very company that he had co-founded.

Would it be preposterous to conclude that Land's ego had catalysed his toppling?

Land saw himself as a physicist and a chemist, and for three decades, these identities powered his brilliant ideas, actions, and inventions that resulted in his great run. But when the digital era started making its irrepressible headway, it was high time for him to let go of these identities in the larger interest of the company. Instead, his ego was unwilling and defensive, precipitating his downfall.

The Ego's Defence Team

The defence team of ahankara, has two players: *mann* and *buddhi*. Mann, often translated as "mind," is the emotional part of our psyche. And buddhi, often translated as "intelligence," is the rational part. Mann, buddhi, and ahankara together form our *sukshma sharir*, our "invisible self" or "psyche." (Interestingly, even according to modern science, our psyche consists of three selves: the emotional self, the rational self, and the egoistic self.)

The mind acts as the ego's hatchet man and one of its jobs is to keep the ego happy. Any information coming in from the senses that threaten any identity given by the ego, the mind dismisses. It expresses this rejection through negative feelings like fear, anger, disgust, melancholy, annoyance, and so on. Edwin Land's mind, for example, very likely picked annoyance when Akio Morita expressed that the wave of the future could be digital, a piece of information that threatened Land's identity of being a physicist and a chemist.

Intelligence is the mind's champion; it analyses the situation in accordance with the feelings generated by the mind. When Land was annoyed, his intelligence managed to reason out why the idea of a digital takeover was indeed irksome: people would always want printed photos, and the quality of digital photography would always be substandard.

Coming back to the murder story of Kitty Genovese, the apathy surrounding her slaying had hit Bill hard. He wanted to be empathetic; that was to be his new identity. Empathising with the American cause in Vietnam, therefore, became his calling. While defending that identity of being empathetic, his ego presumably ignored the naysayers of the Vietnam War, just as Land ignored Morita's foresight.

Bill's story is a stark example of how the ego's tendency to defend identities can be a detriment even with virtues like empathy. It also demonstrates how the ego can have an overbearing influence on your life—unbeknownst to you—even though you qualify nowhere close to being labelled an egomaniac.

Further Implications of the Ego's Reluctance to Let Go

The ego's reluctance to let go of identities has ramifications on every world that you inhabit—from the macro to the micro.

So far we have only been discussing the ego-driven undoing of the lives and careers of individuals. Before we move on, here's another interesting case that I came across as a spiritual life coach: that of a young man who relentlessly held onto the identity of being a professional cricketer. He spent hours at the net practising and dreamed of making his mark on the international scene one day. Blindsided by his ego, he ignored the raw reality that he hadn't even qualified for first-class cricket despite his advancing age. Clearly, it was high time for him to pivot away from the sport and start looking for alternative careers. But he was struggling to let go of his cherished identity even as time was ticking by, leaving him with fewer and fewer backup career options. I have seen this trend extend beyond the cricket ground, to people repeatedly attempting—but failing—to gain a CA degree, an IAS post, or a role in Bollywood. The list is endless.

On the global stage, the ego's reluctance to let go of identities has been the steadfast recipe for wars all through history. While World War I got instigated and extended because countries couldn't let go of their extreme nationalism, World War II was founded on Nazis defending a fabricated identity that Hitler had given them. And as regards the annals of wars that followed, the same principle of defending identities beyond limits resurfaces as the root cause time and time again. Right now, as I am typing these words on my computer, China is rehearsing military drills for the invasion of Taiwan, with the intent of defending its "One China" identity.

And while this war-mongering continues between nations, small domestic battles are being waged in innumerable Indian homes between mothers-in-law and daughters-in-law, again because of the ego's tendency to hold on to expired identities. In Sanskrit, a mother's affection for her son is called *mamata,* which means "ownership." The mother has the identity of being the owner of her son, and it sure enhances the sweetness of motherhood. But once the son gets married, a new owner enters his life: his wife. And if the mother fails to acknowledge this change in proprietorship and continues to defend her expired identity, a war is sparked in the household.

Even in nuclear families, it's often because of the ego that couples grow apart. Husbands and wives end up drawing battlelines upon returning from office because they refuse to leave behind their professional identities at the doormat. You may be the boss at the office, but back home your identity gets relegated to that of a servant—doesn't matter whether you are the husband or the wife. Either you acknowledge this and learn to play the part or prepare yourself for fireworks.

Zooming into the run-of-the-mill affairs of your daily life, whenever you feel stressed or anxious, it's very likely the ego that is stoking these negative emotions. Let's suppose that your ego has given you the identity that you are good-looking. Now, if the evening selfie that you posted on Instagram is starving for likes even late in the night, you will very likely go to bed anxiety-ridden and stressed out. Waking up in the morning, if you find it still famished, you will be either depressed, or angry at your friends, at the world, or perhaps at yourself. On the other hand, if your post is brimming with likes by morning, you will likely get arrogant. Or at least, your identity of being good-looking will get reinforced. There would be little reason to celebrate, though, because the next time you post your selfie on Instagram—with that heightened conviction about your good looks—your experience is going to be more intense and stressful, to begin with, and then, either more painful or boastful. When the ego wins a battle, prepare for the war that's going to follow; and if it wins again, prepare for a bigger war. The more wars it wins, the more excruciating will be the defeat that eventually follows.

When the ego battles to defend an identity, you experience stress and anxiety; when it loses, you slip into depression or soar into a rage; and when it wins, you become arrogant. This battle within is waged every single day, every now and again. These emotions—stress, anxiety, anger, depression, and arrogance—are ubiquitous in our times, a primary reason being that people's egos are busy defending identities all day long.

On the professional front too, your efficiency will plummet if you don't learn to let go of identities. Let's examine a professional tennis player's life to gain more clarity on this point. In his memoir *Rafa*, the legendary Rafael Nadal says, "What I battle hardest to do in a tennis match is to quiet the voices in my head… and concentrate every atom of my being on the point I am playing. If I made a mistake on a previous point, forget it; should a thought of victory suggest itself, crush it." Those "voices in the head" that Nadal is talking about are from the ego's defence team. When you encounter a setback, the ego quickly hands you the identity of being a loser; when you see success on the horizon, the ego promptly awards you the identity of being a winner. Either way, its defence team jumps on board to defend the identity, filling your head with "voices" that don't allow you to concentrate on the task at hand, thus draining you of your efficiency.

In his book, Nadal documents in detail his struggle with the "voices" in his head as he played through the historic 2008 Wimbledon Final against another tennis giant, Roger Federer.

In the very first set of the match, when Nadal broke Federer's serve to gain a two-game-to-one lead, the TV commentator exclaimed, "What a break of serve it is! First blood to the Spaniard (Nadal) in his attempt to win Wimbledon for the first time." Nadal, however, "felt satisfied but not elated," as he discloses in his autobiography. "There was a long road ahead, and any thought of victory, any hint now of a movie with a happy ending entering my head, would have been suicide." In other words, Nadal didn't allow his ego to prematurely crown him with the identity of being a winner. Having outplayed Federer, and more importantly his own ego, Nadal went on to win the first set 6–4. And then the second. "The scoreboard said I was two sets to love up, but in my mind it was still 0–0," writes Nadal, "One set away from winning Wimbledon, people watching might have felt I was within easy reach of my life's dream. But I intended to allow no such thoughts into my head. I would take each point as it came, in isolation. I'd forget everything else, obliterate the future and the past, exist only in the moment."

During the seventh game of the third set, Nadal succumbed to the ego—nearly. The scores levelled at three-games-all, and with Federer serving, Nadal secured three break points. But then he lost all three. In the face of disappointment, the formidable ego posed a test... "and I failed it, that's why I remember it so painfully," he recalls. "I failed where I had trained myself all my life to be strongest. And once again, I caught myself thinking, 'I may not get this chance again; this might be the turning point of the match.'" In other words, his ego had sold him the identity that he was already a loser, and he had bought it. But before the ego's defence team could cloud his head with its voices, he "wiped out" that identity from his head "immediately". And so, his play remained unaffected. Regardless, Federer elevated his own game and won the set.

In the fourth set, Nadal was 5–2 up in the tie-break, two points away from the championship, when he allowed himself a moment of celebration. "Nothing too exuberant, nothing the Centre Court crowd could see," writes Nadal, "but inside—I couldn't help myself—I felt this was nearly, nearly it. Serving, at 5–2 up, I felt I was within touching distance of my life's dream. And that was my downfall." This time the ego had successfully bestowed upon him—prematurely—the identity of being the Wimbledon champion, and the mind and intelligence had been whipped up into defence mode. His embattled mind became stressed and anxious—almost instantly. Nadal records in his memoir: "Until now, the adrenaline had beaten the nerves; now suddenly the nerves trumped all. I felt as if I were on the edge of a precipice." Even before he had climbed to the summit, his mind was ironically gripped with the fear of falling off the "cliff of glory". And what about his intelligence? Taking a cue from the mind's fear, it started to overanalyse the situation: "As I bounced the ball up and down before my first serve, I thought, 'Where should I hit it? Should I be brave and aim at his (Federer's) body, trying to catch him by surprise, even though I failed with that gambit a couple of sets back?' I shouldn't have given it so much thought." The voices in his head winning over him, Nadal lost the next three points, and eventually the fourth set, to Federer.

"It's a rotten feeling to be so close to your goals and have it taken away," you can hear the commentator empathising with Nadal if you watch this match on YouTube. As the camera focuses on the young Spaniard sitting on his chair waiting for the final set to begin, the commentator adds, "He must feel hollow, absolutely hollow." But that conjecture couldn't have been farther from the truth.

"As I sat in my chair waiting for the set to begin," writes Nadal in his memoir, "I wasn't lamenting the loss of the last two sets, I wasn't letting my failure to capitalise on the 5–2 advantage I had on the last tiebreak eat me up." If not for his alertness, the ego would have again promoted—this time—the identity that he was a loser. And the voices in his head would have returned.

In summary, underpinning the extraordinary success of Nadal is his ability to let go of the identities that the ego relentlessly keeps imposing upon him all through a tennis match: either that he is a winner, or that he is a loser. And you stand to learn much from him, even if the fluctuations you experience in your profession may not be nearly as frequent and turbulent as Nadal's.

And Nadal's uncle Toni, who coached his nephew since childhood, has advice for parents, which is again related to the ego. "The problem nowadays," he says, "is that children have become too much the centre of attention. Their parents, their families, everyone around them feels a need to put them on a pedestal. So much effort is invested in boosting their self-esteem that they are made to feel special in and of themselves, without having done anything... they fail to grasp that you are not special because of who you are but because of what you do."

Such children continue to feel entitled even when they grow up, for the identities entrenched in childhood are the hardest to let go of in adulthood.

"I see it all the time," continues Toni. "And then, if it turns out that they make money and acquire a little fame and everything is made easy for them and no one ever contradicts them, they are accommodated in every little detail of life, well ... you end up with the most unbearable spoiled brats."

The Bhagavad Gita Begins with Arjuna's Ego Becoming Defensive

Interestingly, the Bhagavad Gita opens with the warrior Arjuna—his ego rather—trying to defend identities on the battlefield of Kurukshetra.

The lead-up to this fratricidal war is described in the epic Mahabharata. The Kauravas—one hundred brothers headed by Duryodhana—had usurped the throne belonging to their cousins, the Pandava brothers—Yudhishtira, Bhima, Arjuna, Nakula, and Sahadeva. Consequently, the citizens suffered under the sinister rule of Duryodhana, a megalomaniac. The Pandavas, after failing to negotiate a peaceful settlement, had rightfully decided to wage a war to reclaim their kingdom—not for themselves, but for *dharma*, or "righteousness", to prevail in the state. Meanwhile, Duryodhana, continuing with his trickery, had convinced a significant portion of the family, friends, and kinsmen to side with him during the fight against the Pandavas.

At the brink of war, Arjuna lost his nerve. He turned to his charioteer, Lord Sri Krishna:

> My dear Krishna, seeing my friends and relatives present before me in such a fighting spirit, I feel the limbs of my body quivering and my mouth drying up... I do not see how any good can come from killing my kinsmen in this battle... why should I wish to kill them, even though they might otherwise kill me? (Bhagavad Gita 1.29, 31, 34)

On the battlefield, opposing Arjuna, were figures like grandfather Bhishma, whose presence reminded Arjuna of his own identity as a beloved grandson. There was Guru Drona, whose presence brought to his mind his duties as an obedient disciple; friend Ashvatthama's presence evoked his commitment as a loyal friend; uncle Shalya's sight called upon his responsibility as a caring nephew. The prospect of war threatened all these identities—of being a cherished grandson, a compliant disciple, a trustworthy friend, a loving nephew, and many others. As a result, Arjuna's ego kicked into defense mode, and his mind was flooded with negative feelings of depression, as reflected in Arjuna's words.

Next, Arjuna's intelligence backed up those feelings with rationalisations; the Gita lists—verse after verse—the reasons he gave in favour of avoiding war.

Sri Krishna, recognising Arjuna's state of mind, dismissed those feelings and justifications. It was high time that Arjuna let go of those identities and fulfilled his duty as a responsible warrior. Sri Krishna did not mince his words while shaking up Arjuna:

> Do not yield to this degrading impotence. It does not become you. Give up such petty weakness of heart and arise, O chastiser of the enemy. (Bhagavad Gita 2.3)

Sri Krishna didn't stop at this, for he knew a mere pep-talk would fall short as Arjuna's crisis ran deep—it was rooted in the ego.

Sri Krishna subsequently mentored Arjuna in the art of letting go of identities through Karma Yoga.

*

The Bhagavad Gita comprises 18 *Adhyaayas* or "chapters". The first Adhyaaya primarily contains Arjuna's reasons for not fighting. Adhyaayas 2 to 5 are exclusively about Karma Yoga. This book draws from these Adhyaayas.

Karma Yoga, in essence, is about leading a purpose-driven life.

The first part of this book touches upon the correlation between being purposeful and the art of letting go. The second part elaborates on how to elevate yourselves to become purpose-driven. For, although there's a lot of buzz nowadays about being purposeful, hardly anyone seems to know how to get there except the Gita. The third part of this book analyses what's a worthy purpose worth dedicating your lives to; again an important issue that most moderns don't think through. The fourth part is about tips for furthering your advancement in Karma Yoga. And the fifth part details how to let go, after situating yourself firmly as a Karma Yogi.

Part one of this book maps to Adhyaaya 2 of the Gita; parts two and three map to Adhyaaya 3; and parts four and five to Adhyaayas 4 and 5 respectively.

PART I

The Subtle Art of Letting Go

1

THE ART OF LETTING GO – I
Through Saankhya

"Congratulation Sri Lanka, we're sorry." This grammatically incorrect sentence brought solace to millions of cricket lovers across India on March 13, 1996. That evening at the Eden Gardens stadium in Kolkata, spectators supporting the Indian cricket team had shamefully rioted and disrupted the match when their side was on the brink of defeat against the Sri Lankans in the World Cup semi-finals. Match referee Clive Lloyd, after a failed attempt at calming the crowds, had awarded the match to Sri Lanka. From the stands, a lone Indian soul had braved to display a placard with the aforementioned words of true sportsmanship—rightfully congratulating the Lankans and apologising for all the misconduct happening around.

The mishap at Eden Gardens, for the most part, can be considered a one-off, a rare anomaly. To let go is relatively easy for spectators, though it remains a formidable challenge for most players, as we discussed in the introduction.

Even for champions—of the ilk of Nick Kyrgios and Novak Djokovic in tennis, and Duncan Ferguson and Vinnie Jones in soccer—losing their cool during the course of a match isn't uncommon. At first glance, this disparity in response to upheavals between those on and off the field seems obvious: after all, those sweating it out in the middle have a lot more at stake—the reward of winning. But could there be more to it than meets the eye? For an answer, we foray into a world far from sports, where people don't struggle to let go on cricket fields or tennis courts, but in their finely furnished cubicles.

A Story about Letting Go from the Business World

Let's examine the case study of software genius Avie Tevanian, the famed developer at Apple, who let go of his rights at a health technology corporation called Theranos, but not without an initial struggle.

Avie's stint with Theranos had begun with his investment of $1.5 million in shares and joining the company's board as director. He had met the CEO and co-founder Elizabeth Holmes, who had come across to him as an upbeat, passionate, and promising young entrepreneur. Holmes also seemed to be fascinated by Avie because of his old and close association with Steve Jobs.

But before long, the relationship soured. Once on board, Avie was quick to notice Holmes's inability to deliver anything beyond dreamy promises. Under her leadership, the company seemed to be heading nowhere. On top of that, she was keen on cementing her veto power in the corporation, something that Avie thought would go against the company's interests and those of the shareholders'. He objected, and Holmes pushed back.

Through the board's chairman, Holmes conveyed her displeasure to Avie and proposed that he resign. At first, he was taken aback: why was he being restricted from doing his duty as a responsible board member? Then he paused and thought it over. He wasn't interested in conflict, and so agreed to quit the board. But before Avie could ease himself out, the next shocker arrived—Holmes wanted him to sign a waiver:

The de facto co-founder of the startup, Shaunak Roy, had decided to call it quits, and his shares were up for grabs. Holmes, sprinting into action, had first influenced the board to waive the company's rights to acquire those shares; then she had promptly negotiated a sweetheart deal with Roy for acquiring all of that stock personally. Now, for her scheme to reach the finish line, Avie was asked to sign a waiver waiving his own rights to acquire the pro-rata portion of Roy's shares to which he was entitled as a shareholder. This time, however, Avie was reluctant to let go.

Matters began to escalate when Theranos's general counsel accused Avie of publicly disparaging the company and threatened him with legal consequences should he fail to sign the waiver. Avie could neither make sense of the false accusations nor of the unlawful lawsuit.

Unsure what to do, he contacted a friend who was a lawyer. After hearing Avie out, the friend asked a question that helped Avie put the situation in perspective: "Given everything you know about this company, do you really want to own more of it?" When Avie thought about it, the answer was "no". Having served on the Theranos board and having been its major shareholder, Avie had grown to identify himself as one of the company's owners. Unthinkingly, he was trying to defend that identity—and even deepen it—by buying more of its shares. His friend had now shaken him out of that stupor: under Elizabeth Holmes's leadership, Theranos was clearly headed for doom—and so it no longer made sense to hold on to the identity of being its proprietor. To let go was clearly the way forward. And that meant not buying those shares, let alone vying for them.

When you realise an identity is of no consequence in the long run, adopting a detached perspective becomes easier, making letting go a lesser ordeal.

Returning to the world of sports, letting go is easier for spectators because they recognise the identities they assume while watching a match as temporary. For instance, I identify myself as a Nadal fan as I watch him play, and I do identify myself as a loser whenever he loses, but quietly I understand the irrelevance of those identities beyond the span of the game. On the other hand, for a player—especially a professional player like Nadal—the identity of being a loser or a winner remains relevant way beyond the game. After all, tennis is his vocation. "My defeat in 2007, which went to five sets, left me utterly destroyed," Nadal reveals in his memoir his mental state after Federer had given him a crushing defeat in the 2007 Wimbledon final. "My uncle Toni, the toughest of tennis coaches, is usually the last person in the world to offer me consolation; he criticises me even when I win. It is a measure of what a wreck I must have been that he abandoned the habit of a lifetime and told me there was no reason to cry, that there would be more Wimbledons and more Wimbledon finals. I told him he didn't understand, that this had probably been my last time here, my last chance to win it... and I cannot bear the thought of squandering an opportunity that might never come again." Note that Nadal's justification for not letting go reflected a sense of permanence he had attached to the identity of being a loser at Wimbledon.

That Nadal eventually bounced back in 2008 to lift the trophy despite being "haunted by the recollection of defeat in 2007" makes him a towering champion of our times. For most players, it's hard to put a crushing defeat as significant as that behind them. And for many, even a point lost at the end of a well-played rally could be demoralising. In essence, letting go of a loss is harder for a professional player because it seems consequential even in the long run.

And the same principle holds true in any profession, or for that matter, in any walk of life: the more you see an identity as permanent, the harder it will be to let go of it.

Conversely, letting go will be much easier if you learn to see how every identity—no matter how long-lasting it may seem at the moment—has absolutely no bearing in the grand scheme of things.

In Reality, Nothing Is Permanent

In his recently published book, author Mark Manson imagines working at Starbucks. At the coffeehouse, instead of writing people's names on their coffee cup, he wants to write them a message. Here's an excerpt from his intended note to all customers:

"One day, you and everyone you love will die. And beyond a small group of people for an extremely brief period of time, little of what you say or do will ever matter... We are inconsequential cosmic dust, bumping and milling about on a tiny blue speck. We imagine our own importance."

If you ponder over the lines above, Manson couldn't be more correct.

His first line—"one day, you and everyone you love is going to die"—is an indisputable truth. Our identification with our body is indeed transient. It's only a matter of time before this amalgamation of flesh, blood, and bones disintegrates into, what he calls, "inconsequential cosmic dust." And since our bodies are temporary, so are our identities regarding bodily relationships.

As for "what you say or do," isn't it true that all of that becomes immaterial "beyond a small group of people"? Even the cricketing legend Sachin Tendulkar is no exception to this truth. His batting heroics were largely irrelevant to the non-cricketing world; indeed, most people in those countries haven't even heard of him. Notably, during a post-match press conference at Wimbledon in 2014, when the Russian tennis star Maria Sharapova was asked by a reporter if she knew him, her blunt reply was, "I don't know of Sachin Tendulkar." She was clueless about the "world-renowned" batter who had watched her play from the Royal Box at Centre Court, while in the same breath she acknowledged the presence of another sports star, David Beckham, who had sat alongside Tendulkar watching the same match (now if you are caught wondering who Beckham is, he is a football legend who is irrelevant beyond the soccer-playing world).

Secondly, wouldn't it be accurate to say that a significant portion of "what you say or do" is relevant only "for an extremely brief period of time"? Edwin Land, whom we met in the introduction, was a monumental tech icon of the twentieth century. (In fact, Steve Jobs considered him one of his role models.) Land contributed significantly to the world of photography between the 1940s and 80s. But fast-forward just four decades, and his lifetime of work seems obsolete. How many photographers of today use the cameras or film invented by him? Or for that matter, how many people now remember him? Ironically, if you had even heard his name prior to reading this book, you have handily beaten the odds.

And so, if your words and actions won't hold up in the face of infinite space and eternal time, how can the identities that define them feature in the bigger picture of things? Despite this apparent reality, we get so caught up in the minutiae of everyday life that the impermanence that surrounds every one of our identities—whether personal or professional—is lost on us.

And if only we could resist this tendency towards myopia, nurturing a detached perspective would be much easier, and letting go less burdensome.

All that said, focusing too much on the transience of things can have its pitfalls too. Recently, I displayed Manson's words quoted above on the big screen during a parenting seminar that I conducted. My idea was to equip parents to help their teenage children let go of failures. No sooner had the LCD projector flashed Manson's quote than a father timidly raised his hand, "Well, my son may say that if everything is impermanent, life is meaningless. He might even go to the extent of asking—what's the point of living?" That was a valid concern, and I had seen it coming. Manson does address this issue in his book, but in his own distinct way. Instead, I chose the time-tested course of the Gita to placate the rattled parent.

The Gita Offsets Impermanence with Permanence

Returning to the battlefield of Kurukshetra, when Arjuna was struggling to let go of his various identities—a pet grandson, an obedient disciple, a faithful friend, a loving nephew and so on—Lord Krishna initially berated Arjuna as being weak-hearted and urged him to fight. When that didn't work, Lord Krishna pinpointed to Arjuna the temporary nature of the body and all bodily relationships. His intent was to invoke a sense of detachment in Arjuna, to help Arjuna let go. But interestingly, Lord Krishna intertwined those talks of the impermanence of everything material with the description of what's permanent—the spirit soul within the body. He pitted spirit against matter, an analysis technically called *Saankhya*.

> Those who are seers of the truth have concluded that of the nonexistent [the material body] there is no endurance and of the eternal [the soul] there is no change. This they have concluded by studying the nature of both. (Bhagavad Gita 2.16)

That which pervades the entire body you should know to be indestructible. No one is able to destroy that imperishable soul. (Bhagavad Gita 2.17)

The material body of the indestructible, immeasurable and eternal living entity, on the other hand, is sure to come to an end; therefore, fight, O descendant of Bharata. (Bhagavad Gita 2.18)

It is said that the soul is invisible, inconceivable, and immutable. Knowing this, you should not grieve for the body. (Bhagavad Gita 2.25)

One who has taken his birth is sure to die, and after death, one is sure to take birth again. Therefore, in the unavoidable discharge of your duty, you should not lament. (Bhagavad Gita 2.27)

Why did Lord Krishna have to speak of the "imperishable" and the "indestructible"? By emphasising the eternality of the soul, he aimed for two objectives. Firstly, he reassured Arjuna that his enemies would be deathless even if he laid them dead, thus appealing to Arjuna's sense of compassion. Secondly, and more importantly, he lifted the curtain on the spiritual dimension of life, thus sparing Arjuna an identity crisis.

If Lord Krishna had only stripped open the stark reality of the material dimension—how everything is ultimately temporary—that would have evoked detachment in Arjuna for sure, but also left him in limbo. Struggling to find a grip over a life full of slippery identities, he would have perhaps wondered—"If everything is impermanent, life is hopeless. In fact, what's the point of doing anything?" Arjuna would have suffered—what is often termed in the modern-day world—

"identity crisis". That was the last thing Lord Krishna was asking for. Therefore, no sooner had he closed-shut for Arjuna all hope in material identities than he promptly handed him a spiritual identity that, being eternal, opened up an undying dimension of hope.

Following in the footsteps of Lord Krishna, I too presented this spiritual alternative to the concerned father in the parenting seminar. Nonetheless, he retorted, "My son may say that if being a soul is our only eternal identity, we may well drop all our material responsibilities and become sannyasis!"

Letting Go Doesn't Mean Letting Go Indiscriminately

Most people struggle to understand that awareness of the impermanence of material identities and the sense of detachment it evokes, does not necessarily imply that they must let go of them prematurely. You let go of a material identity only when it reaches its expiry date.

For instance, in Arjuna's case, his identities connected to his relationships had expired, and it was time to let go of them. But if he let go of his identity of being a warrior on a battlefield, that would be nothing short of catastrophic; and Lord Krishna made sure to drive home this point in a series of verses:

> Considering your specific duty as a kṣatriya, you should know that there is no better engagement for you than fighting on religious principles; and so there is no need for hesitation. (Bhagavad Gita 2.31)

O Partha, happy are the kṣatriyas to whom such fighting opportunities come unsought, opening for them the doors of the heavenly planets. (Bhagavad Gita 2.32)

If, however, you do not perform your religious duty of fighting, then you will certainly incur bad karma for neglecting your duties and thus lose your reputation as a fighter. (Bhagavad Gita 2.33)

People will always speak of your infamy, and for a respectable person, dishonor is worse than death. (Bhagavad Gita 2.34)

The great generals who have highly esteemed your name and fame will think that you have left the battlefield out of fear only, and thus they will consider you insignificant. (Bhagavad Gita 2.35)

Your enemies will describe you in many unkind words and scorn your ability. What could be more painful for you? (Bhagavad Gita 2.36)

O son of Kunti, either you will be killed on the battlefield and attain the heavenly planets, or you will conquer and enjoy the earthly kingdom. Therefore, get up with determination and fight. (Bhagavad Gita 2.37)

No sooner had I explained all these than another parent interjected with a query: "How do we know which identity has expired and which hasn't?" Hearing that, I glowed from within. The interactive seminar was following the script, and the stage was now set for me to introduce yoga: the art of firmly situating ourselves on the spiritual platform, which empowers us to clearly distinguish the material identities that have expired from those that haven't.

2

THE ART OF LETTING GO – II
Through Yoga

On March 13, 1996, as the Indian cricket team was battling against Sri Lanka at the Eden Gardens stadium, I was watching the match live on television. I too was glued to the screen when Tendulkar and Manjrekar were building a second-wicket partnership. But then Tendulkar was stumped, followed by six more batters falling in quick succession. With eight wickets down and the score languishing at 120, the Indian team was suddenly running on fumes. That's when the spectators at Eden Gardens caused an uproar. But I had neither the time to brood nor to bawl over India's imminent loss. Strewn all around me in heaps were academic books demanding my urgent attention, reminding me of my 12th standard board exam that was knocking—nay, thumping—at the door. I promptly turned off the television and immersed myself in my studies.

As we discussed in the previous chapter, I could brush aside my team's defeat because I saw my identity as its fan as temporary. But that's just a partial explanation. A more comprehensive analysis of my story will help you understand how a yogi lets go of material identities as and when they expire.

Let's Begin By Defining Yoga

This is how Lord Krishna defines yoga in the Bhagavad Gita:

> Perform your duty equipoised, O Arjuna, abandoning all attachment to success or failure. Such equanimity is called yoga. (Bhagavad Gita 2.48)

And this is what it essentially means: yoga is all about situating oneself firmly in the identity of being a spirit soul.

Let me explain.

Referring back to my response to India's World Cup loss, I could remain equipoised only because I was firmly situated in the identity of being a student. Back in the day, everyone in India regarded the board exam as pivotal in a youngster's life-journey; in terms of the impact it had on one's future, it rivalled the Last Judgment in Christian theology—at least that's what parents and teachers impressed upon us. In retrospect, all of that hype was a grand fairytale. Regardless, we all bought it, and I took my exam extremely seriously. It was as if I was born with a mathematics book in hand, and my body was destined to be cremated on a pyre of piled books—physics, chemistry, and the like. In essence, the spectre of the board exam made the identity of being a student seem so permanent that the identity of being a fan of the Indian cricket team felt temporary in comparison.

Consequently, I was viewing that match between India and Sri Lanka with a sense of detachment. I was knee-deep into the match, but never neck-deep; I was engrossed, but never lost. And so, when the scene turned apocalyptic at Eden Gardens, I could wade out of the waters with ease. I turned away from the television, and towards my "permanent" identity of being a student.

In the run-up to the semi-finals, when India had won several matches, was my response any different? No. I had my nose in a textbook on every occasion, rather than wasting excess time in celebration.

In the same vein as the ostensibly permanent identity of being a student helped me navigate through India's failures and successes, Arjuna's firm grounding in the genuinely permanent identity of being a spirit soul would keep him equipoised on the battlefield. To the extent he identified himself as a soul, he would perceive the warrior-identity as temporary in comparison, and could view the ups and downs on the battlefield with a sense of detachment. So that was what yoga meant for Arjuna, and that's what yoga is for everybody: situating firmly in the permanent identity of being an *atma,* to an extent that all material identities unconsciously seem temporary.

Yoga Doesn't Mean Irresponsibility Regarding Material Duties

Watching the match between India and Sri Lanka from arm's length provided me with a clearer view of a reality that—I would wager—was lost on most spectators. Even as the game turned nerve-shredding, I was conscious all the while that I had no control over how the players played, and therefore absolutely no say in who would win or who would lose.

That's not to say that I wasn't cheering and praying like any dutiful Indian fan. When Sanath Jayasuriya, the firebrand opener of the Sri Lankan team, fell early during the match, a thrill did course through my veins; when Tendulkar was in full flow, cruising past his half-century, I too was over the moon; and I was holding out hope for my team to win against all odds until the very end. Without experiencing those scintillating emotions and the glow of wild optimism, what was the point of being a spectator in the first place? The whole objective—of entertainment—would be defeated.

In essence, the situation demanded of me a delicate balancing act—between being a dutiful Indian fan and a detached spectator.

Arjuna's challenge would be to juggle his identity of being a dutiful warrior with that of being a detached soul.

By anchoring himself in yoga, in the identity of being a soul, Arjuna would surely gain a clearer understanding of how innumerable factors beyond him stood to contribute towards the outcome of the war. Yoga—because it elevates one's consciousness—provides a bird's-eye view of the material plane below, and with it, a better picture of how little control one has over the results of one's activities.

Interestingly, this yogic insight—which contradicts the materialistic tendency of accepting all the praise or blame for the outcome of one's endeavours—is gradually gaining acceptance even in academia. Take, for instance, what Assistant Professor Gautam Mukunda of Harvard Business School has to say:

> It's way too easy to think, 'I've always succeeded, I am a success, I am successful because I am a success, because it's about me...' Wrong. You were successful because you happened to be in an environment where your biases, predispositions, talents, and abilities all happened to align neatly with those things that would produce success in that environment. (*Barking Up the Wrong Tree*, Eric Barker).

Mukunda highlights here only the contribution of the immediate environment. Through yoga, Arjuna could also perceive—all in good time—more subtle and remote contributors like *devas* and karma, to name only a few.

But that's not to say that he was granted leeway for being a sloppy warrior. The situation called for war, and he couldn't be effective as a warrior without being responsible. And so, Lord Krishna urged him to perform a delicate act of balance.

> You have a right to perform your prescribed duty, but that alone doesn't entitle you to the fruits of action. You are never the sole cause of the results of your activities, but never be attached to not doing your duty. (Bhagavad Gita 2.47)

Yoga Is about Sharpening Your Spiritual Convictions

Returning to my story of primarily identifying myself as a student, a great deal of rational thought was invested in that decision. Throughout my high school days, my parents and teachers emphasised stories of students who excelled in their board exams, subsequently gaining admission into top-tier professional colleges. After graduation, they were either absorbed by overseas universities or recruited by multinational corporations (MNCs). This was indeed an observable fact. The argument that the board exam sets the pace for your entire future seemed intellectually sound. Thus, with that intellectual conviction, I prioritised the identity of being a student for an entire year. (Of course, later in life, I met many people who were highly successful despite their 12th standard scores, which led me to no longer uphold the common perception that board exams are as crucial as they are portrayed).

Even when it comes to firmly identifying yourself as an atma, it will be significantly easier if you are rationally convinced that you are indeed an immortal soul encased within a mortal body. Thanks to a relatively recent surge of scientific studies, thousands of cases of reincarnation, out-of-body experiences (OBEs), and near-death experiences (NDEs) have been empirically verified.[1] You need only familiarise yourself with these findings—and as your conviction in your spiritual identity deepens, your identification with your material identities will proportionately lessen.

---

[1] The pioneer among frontline researchers of reincarnation was the late Ian Stevenson, Carlson Professor of Psychiatry and director of the Division of Personality Studies at the University of Virginia. He investigated more than three thousand cases of reincarnation, which he documented in his book *Reincarnation and Biology: A Contribution to the Etiology of Birthmarks and Birth Defects*.

When you cross the dense forest of material delusion through your intelligence, you shall become indifferent to all that has been heard and all that is to be heard (regarding mundane identities). (Bhagavad Gita 2.52)

Yoga Is about Experiencing Higher Spiritual Emotions

As life coach Tony Robbins puts it, "Emotion is the force of life." If this weren't true, companies could save millions in advertising budgets by having nerds from their research labs read out the distinguishing features of their products on television in scientific jargon. Instead, they employ flashy movie stars and fervent sports stars who are paid to flaunt the product while energetically dancing and dashing across the screen, without uttering a word about the product itself. We may be reluctant to admit this, but in reality, our decision-making is powered more by the heart than by the head.

So yes, my reasoning did play a role in putting India's world cup loss behind me and getting back to my studies. However, what truly eased my letting go was my penchant for solving physics problems and balancing chemical equations—believe it or not. Meanwhile, India's cricket captain, Mohammad Azharuddin, found a different way to overcome the World Cup hangover. Allegedly, just two days after that devastating defeat against Sri Lanka, Azhar was spotted with his new love, Sangeeta Bijlani, in the misty gardens of Kodaikanal, a far cry from the mayhem at Eden Gardens.

Letting go is always easier when you have something better and bigger—emotionally—to hold on to.

For another example, let's briefly revisit the story of Avie Tevanian, whom we met in the previous chapter. At the time when his lawyer friend talked him into introspection, his personal balance sheet was larger than that of Theranos's—thanks to the money he had made at Apple earlier. Without that substantial bank balance, could he have adopted such a detached stance on Theranos, despite knowing its inside story intellectually? The answer is anyone's guess.

Sachin Tendulkar, in the first chapter of his autobiography *Playing It My Way*, quotes his father's words that enabled him to let go of successes throughout his career: "Do not allow success to breed arrogance in you. If you remain humble, people will give you love and respect even after you have finished with the game. As a parent, I would be happier hearing people say, 'Sachin is a good human being' than 'Sachin is a great cricketer' any day." By attaching himself to the identity of being a good human being—which is emotionally more appealing—Tendulkar could prevent career successes from going to his head.

Yoga, too, involves experiencing higher, supramundane emotions through realising your spiritual identity. This, in turn, helps you transcend mundane emotions, and let go of the material identities that evoke them.

> Yoga isn't about artificially maintaining a detached perspective towards life. An accomplished yogi naturally feels a healthy emotional detachment from the material by experiencing a higher taste that's spiritual. (Bhagavad Gita 2.59)

Yoga Is about Being Purpose-Driven

Let's rewind to the night of March 13, 1996, one last time. As I watched that match between India and Sri Lanka, I knew exactly when to let go of the identity of being an Indian fan: it was when being an Indian fan unbalanced me to such an extent that my studies were on the brink of being adversely affected.

I was driven by a clear purpose—of studying well—which stemmed from the identity of being a student, and that purpose was my yardstick to measure how far to hold on to any of my other identities. The match, to begin with, had provided a much-needed rejuvenating break amid my study marathon. But when the course of events at Eden Gardens began to turn ugly, it was more draining than entertaining for me, and therefore it was decisively the time to exorcise my mind of all fandom.

Similarly, yoga is about being driven by a purpose,[2] which serves as the one-point-focus, the North Star, to decide which material identity to hold on to and which to let go of.

> Those who are on this path are resolute in purpose, and their aim is one. O beloved child of the Kurus, the intelligence of those who are irresolute is many-branched. (Bhagavad Gita 2.41)

But what's that purpose that galvanises a yogi?

---

[2] If karma, or one's assigned duties of life, are used as the means to attain one's purpose, that yoga is termed Karma Yoga. When jnana, philosophical speculation, is used, it's Jnana Yoga. And so on.

Before we explore for an answer, you need to understand the downside of being want-driven. And more importantly, the process that elevates your consciousness from being want-driven to being purpose-driven.

3

MAKING LETTING GO A LESSER ORDEAL
By Adhering to Aparigraha

Growing up, I never missed watching the Miss Universe competition aired on television. But there was something about it that intrigued me year after year: the runner-up never lost her poise, even though she had the hardest time of all the participants—coming so close to the coveted crown, yet having to let it go.

I stopped watching the contest after 2004, the year I joined the monastery. I next heard of it in 2015. A mess-up in the pageant made big news that year. The runner-up, Ariadna Gutierrez of Colombia, I came to know, lost her poise after losing the title. Tearful, her mascara drenched her makeup, and she had to be tended to by fellow participants. The media couldn't stop sympathising with her for days on end. The reason? Towards the end of the competition, as 10 million watched on live television with bated breath, Ariadna was mistakenly declared the winner by host Steve Harvey; the crown was placed on her, and two-odd minutes later, as Ariadna was celebrating on stage, Harvey returned and corrected himself: Pia Alonzo Wurtzbach of the Philippines had actually won and Ariadna Gutierrez was the first runner-up. The crown was taken off Ariadna and placed on Pia.

Ariadna, unlike the runners-up of yesteryears, failed to hide her misery beneath an equipoised façade. Letting go was excruciating for her. But why? Because during that short span, as the crown adorned her head, something had transpired inside her heart: her desire for the title changed from being a want into a need.

Needs are Gluey, and Could Turn Gruesome

"Wants and needs" is a topic I often broach during the seminars I conduct. I start by asking my audience what their needs are. What are the necessities of their life? What do they consider the bare minimum for their well-being? Among the responses, food, shelter and clothing usually come up first. Good health and relationships follow more slowly. Beyond that, hardly anything is mentioned. It's hard to get responses from Indians who tend to be shy in public forums, not to mention their discomfort in expressing their fancier needs to a renounced monk!

My next question vaults their embarrassment to the next level—"What are your wants? Once your list of needs is tended to, what's more on your wish-list?" As expected, blank stares meet me. Then some, the braver ones, timidly admit—a fancy car, a high-end residence, an expensive gadget, and so on.

"Where do the internet and smartphones fit? Do you count them as wants or as needs?" I ask next. Most are honest. "Needs," they confess.

"But was that the case a few years ago? Were the internet or the smartphone necessities then?"

"No. They weren't necessities then. But now they are."

"They were your wants at some point. But now they have become your needs. Wants transform into needs. The wants of today become the needs of tomorrow," I conclude.

If your wish-list is full of wants, you should be concerned. Because once a want evolves—or rather devolves—into a need, it becomes harder to let it go, as was seen in Ariadna's case.

The fallout of the 2015 Miss Universe fiasco, however, was relatively harmless, compared to what happened at Theranos—when its CEO's want devolved into a need.

Elizabeth Holmes launched her entrepreneurial journey wanting to revolutionise the medical industry. Her idea was to have a drop of blood from a fingertip in one prick reveal much more about a person's health than a syringe-full of blood painfully drawn from the person's arm could. It was indeed a revolutionary concept! Soon, it was the talk of the town in Silicon Valley. Holmes's charisma fuelled her fiery idea, and her startup engulfed funding in the millions. Then billions. Theranos' rise was meteoric.

The story is so far so good. But then something happened.

Elizabeth Holmes went from being a positive role model to a negative one when her desire to change the medical industry became an obsessive need. It didn't matter that Theranos' technology was nowhere close to realising her dream of pinprick diagnosis; she scaled up the production of her flawed machines and installed them in shopping malls across the United States. Patients queued up for blood tests, unaware that the results would only be accurate if they were fortunate. It was a full-blown scandal, and when finally exposed, Theranos plummeted from being a $10 billion company to nothing. Lawsuits were thrown at Holmes, and she was sentenced to over 11 years in prison.

Such stories are commonplace in the corporate space, albeit not all are as grisly:

I know a CEO who saw his company grow tenfold in six years. Witnessing that kind of extraordinary growth subconsciously became his need. Now he heads another corporation that's also great but isn't as expansive—and so, he finds himself always out of sorts, miserable to be precise. Another person I know was a COO whose company got sold off. While looking for another job, he couldn't settle for any role lower than a COO, and the market couldn't fulfil that need of his. He quit the industry and now practises astrology. A third person I know made one crore rupees in a single day in the share market. That became his need, and he has been tirelessly trying to replay that blessed day ever since. But in the process, he has lost three crores in trading.

Needs May Be Unlimited, but Time and Resources are Limited

Wants transforming into needs and then getting sticky—and at times gruesome—is just half the story. Here's the other part: these newly formed needs compete with our already existing needs—the more basic and important ones—for time and resources. Take, for instance, our newly found need for whiling away time on the smartphone. Isn't that stealing away from our relationships in real life? That's just one among a bevy of needs that the gadget is thieving from.

A word is in order here about the maxim "it's lonely at the top". This is how I interpret it—the flamboyant need for success overshadows the fundamental need for connection. People at the top, in their desperation to stay there, don't find the quality time to "climb down"—to meet family and friends, for socialising, or just for holidaying. Then, unable to handle all that stress alone, at times they jump down—literally! Perhaps an example would be V. G. Siddharth, the founder of Café Coffee Day, who committed suicide by plunging into the river Netravathi. He had opened a chain of outlets across the globe for people to share hearts over a coffee break. But as someone pointed out—maybe he himself hadn't found the time to visit one of those cafes to bare out his stressed heart to a confidant.

An old Indian fable dramatises this interplay between wants and needs: One crisp morning, a king felt so charitable that he walked up to his faithful sentry stationed at the palace gate and said, "Run from here as far as you can, as fast as you can. From here until where you reach, all that land will be yours. But you need to return to this exact same spot by sunset. Failing which, you lose all that land that you otherwise stand to gain." Elated, the sentry galloped, but kept in mind that the return sprint had to commence by noon for him to comfortably be back on time.

He covered mile after mile of beautiful landscape, all of which would soon be his! But then, as the clock ticked 12, his greed nudged him to keep running ahead. He succumbed to it, as is the human instinct. Even if he went a little ahead, he reasoned, he could always make up for the lost time by sprinting back faster on the return run.

Little by little, he went farther and farther, deceived by his mind. Finally, when he decided to turn back, he was too late and too tired.

Now he *needed* to run back as much distance as he had *wanted* to acquire. And if he failed, all his labour would be meaningless.

Life for us poses the same puzzle as for that sentry. Far as we may go, *wanting* to achieve more, at the end of the day we *need* to return to the same places that bring us happiness—health, love, relationships, family, friendship, and belonging. But the return path will be longer to the extent we go farther. During the onward journey, we may have *wanted* to cover more distance, but during the return trip, we *need* to trudge back the same stretch. In other words, those *wants* that we ourselves pursued have now transformed into *needs*, which have to be dealt with first, before we can tend to our more basic necessities.

Like that sentry, human instinct is to go so far and for so long—wanting more—that returning seems impossible.

So the Gita warns us against wants.

> A person who is not disturbed by the incessant flow of wants—that enter like rivers into the ocean, which is ever being filled but is always still—can alone achieve peace, and not the person who strives to satisfy such wants. (Bhagavad Gita 2.70)

> A person who has given up all wants, who lives a want-free life, who has given up all sense of proprietorship and is devoid of egoism—alone can attain real peace. (Bhagavad Gita 2.71)

The More the Wants, the Harder It Is to Let Go

With each want that devolves into a need, a new identity is piled atop your already existing heap of material identities. For instance, as Ariadna's desire for the title changed from a want into a need, inside of her emerged the new identity of Miss Universe; as Elizabeth Holmes's passion to revolutionise the medical industry transformed from a want into a need, inside of her was born the new identity of being a Silicon Valley wunderkind. Therefore, the more your wants transform into needs, the more your material identities increase, making letting go a more frequent challenge to grapple with.

Aggressively pursuing wants while simultaneously learning to let go through spirituality is akin to pressing the accelerator while applying the brakes, or fuelling a fire while pouring water on it. Therefore, on the battlefield of Kurukshetra, after briefing Arjuna on the topic of yoga, Sri Krishna broaches *aparigraha*, the "restraint" on the yogic path that beginners should adhere to. To make any tangible progress, neophytes should be wary of wants.

> Those too attached to fulfilling wants are at odds with the spiritual path. (Bhagavad Gita 2.44)

To equip novices with the ability to nip those wants in the bud, the Gita explains their origin.

> While contemplating the objects of the senses, a person develops longing for them, and from such longings wants originate… (Bhagavad Gita 2.62)

> As a strong wind sweeps away a boat on the water, even one of the roaming senses on which the mind focuses can carry away a person's intelligence (into the muddy pool of wants). (Bhagavad Gita 2.67)

> Therefore, O mighty-armed, one whose senses are restrained from their objects is certainly of steady intelligence. (Bhagavad Gita 2.68)

Hearing all this, Arjuna was confused. On one hand, Sri Krishna was advocating yoga, which mandates steering clear of wants, while on the other he was pushing Arjuna to fight a war that seemed want-driven.

> Arjuna asked: O Sri Krishna, why do you want to engage me in this ghastly warfare if you think that restraining my senses is better than actively pursuing wants? My intelligence is bewildered by your equivocal instructions. Therefore, please tell me decisively which will be most beneficial for me. (Bhagavad Gita 3.1, 3.2)

PART II

Going from Want-Driven to Purpose-Driven

4

THE WANT-DRIVEN AND THE PURPOSE-DRIVEN
A Comparison

The time is around seven, the location is New York City, and the date is April 15, 1966. On the top floor of 94 Bowery—which is dirty, dingy, and musty—an elderly Indian swami in his early 70s can be seen lecturing on the Bhagavad Gita. Seated erect and cross-legged on a wooden platform, he criticises the peace proposal made by Arjuna on the battlefield of Kurukshetra. For the swami's audience, a small group of American hippies numbering fewer than a dozen, the names "Arjuna" and "Kurukshetra" ring no bells. But that hardly concerns them. What does concern them, however, are the swami's remarks favouring a battle. Like that ancient warrior named Arjuna, most of them want peace, as do millions of other Americans who oppose their country's involvement in the Vietnam War.

But what exactly was this war in Vietnam about? A detailed and satisfactory answer, even tomes have failed to expound.

So it's pointless to attempt an elaboration here. In essence, however, it was a civil war between the pro-Communists and anti-Communists of Vietnam, with the US actively supporting the latter group. That's just one perspective. Some others see it as a nationalistic war for independence, fought by the Vietnamese—the majority of whom supported communism—against the Americans, who had interfered in a foreign land to support a minority capitalistic group. From yet another stance held by a few, the war was America's noble attempt to stop the spread of communism in Southeast Asia. Regardless of the perspective, the US intervention resulted in millions of lost lives, which was tragic.

The swami's audience—those peaceniks in the Bowery loft—is particularly concerned about President Lyndon Johnson's escalation of America's involvement in the war. Having sent additional troops to Vietnam, Lyndon seems, at least in part, want-driven. A reputed newspaper opined that Lyndon was "a man of towering ambitions" and "he shuddered at the thought of becoming the first president to lose a war." Johnson had ignored a report from the Central Intelligence Agency (CIA) that, in no uncertain terms, denied any necessity to continue the war. The CIA study stated that a defeat in Vietnam wouldn't undermine America's strength, and the damage to national security would be limited and short-lived. In fact, a withdrawal would be perceived as a sign of maturity by other nations. Notwithstanding the CIA report, the president had soldiered on.

Johnson, in retrospect, can't be singled out for having a selfish approach. Every president—from Harry Truman to

Lyndon Johnson—feared the blame for losing in Vietnam. So, they carried on the war legacy, hoping for the next president to bear that blame.

It would be unjust to say that all these presidents were motivated purely by personal interests. They were also concerned about how well the world perceived their nation. But ironically, their war policies in Vietnam ended up portraying the United States as a militarist and imperialist power that was want-driven, bent upon proving its supremacy. American citizens themselves felt guilty of this blemish, as millions of Vietnamese, mostly civilians, lost their lives in US bombings that seemed to serve no end. Overall, America's battle efforts were more self-centred and lacked a selfless drive.

On the other hand, the nationalistic Vietnamese saw their fight against America as a struggle against neocolonialism, a purpose-driven war aimed at freeing their countrymen from foreign oppression. They perceived Americans as opportunistic imperialists who had entered Vietnam following the end of the colonial era of the French and the Japanese.

Being Want-Driven Is Dissatisfying; Being Purpose-Driven Is Satisfying

When you are want-driven, you feel dissatisfied and empty, and what you're doing starts seeming meaningless—especially in the long run. That's how the American war camp felt as the war dragged on for decades. Between 1965 and 1973, 30,000 US troops involved in the Vietnam War were dishonourably discharged for desertion. About half a million men dodged the compulsory war draft that would otherwise have forced them to the battlefront.

While more and more American soldiers felt their nation's intervention as senseless, the Vietcong, the military wing that waged a guerrilla war against the American forces, felt a sense of fulfilment. A French reporter, held hostage for 16 days by the Vietcong, noted their strict discipline. "I saw no evidence to suggest that that discipline was enforced," the journalist wrote. This paradox reveals a high level of self-motivation that results when you are convinced you're doing something meaningful. Despite the absence of draft boards, youngsters aged 15-20 voluntarily flocked to the Vietcong's training camps—ready to lay down their lives for a higher cause.

When you have a purpose that's bigger than you, you enter the realm of selfless service. There, you experience a deep fulfilment and meaning that stems from your very core, from your very soul, because the soul longs to serve unconditionally. This principle is applicable across every sphere of life.

A high-ranking executive of a multibillion-dollar corporation who recently visited our ashram commented to one of my fellow monks: "All that I own is like the vast quantity of water contained in the ocean. As against that, whatever limited possessions you have are akin to the water contained in a well. The ocean water, though unlimited, cannot quench one's thirst, whereas the limited well water can. You utilise whatever little energy and resources you have in selfless service. And that, I reckon, is the cause of your satisfaction, which is evident from your bright and smiling face. I, on the other hand, am always dissatisfied, for I invest my unlimited energy and resources in selfish endeavours." He had eloquently contrasted a purpose-driven life with a want-driven one. And in the process, he brought to life a famous quote by Hollywood star Jim Carrey: "I think everybody should get rich and famous and do everything they ever dreamed of so they can see that it's not the answer."

The Want-Driven are Overwhelmed by Obstacles; the Purpose-Driven Overcome Obstacles

Needless to say, in the absence of inner fulfilment, one is overwhelmed by setbacks and pain. Returning to our discussion on the Vietnam War, the want-driven American side, unable to handle the war pressure, turned to opium and heroin—thousands of soldiers. Some others released their pent-up frustration on their own officers, resulting in hundreds of injuries and deaths. Post-war, half a million Vietnam vets suffered from PTSD (post-traumatic stress disorder).

In contrast, the fulfilment that accompanies a purpose-driven mindset helps you overcome obstacles, setbacks, and pain that you inevitably encounter on the journey towards your goal. That's how Nguyen Thi Do, a nurse with the Vietcong, endured unthinkable hardships. "Some days we had nothing to eat but a fistful of roasted dry rice," she recalls. At one point, their group had to walk through jungles for three and a half months to accomplish a mission. "The leeches were the worst. There were so many of them, all along the way… we didn't even have enough clothes to wear. We walked through the forest all day, and at night. We were hungry the whole way there. Sometimes we had to eat leaves, or roots."

To quote another example—one close to home—I have first-hand witnessed how my purpose-driven sister was able to navigate adversity when, in 2018, my nephew was diagnosed with fourth-stage Chondrosarcoma, a type of soft-tissue cancer. When I visited him in Bengaluru, I saw her tirelessly nurse his deteriorating body, continuously nurture his declining spirit, and endlessly search for a promising doctor, all the while praying to God hopefully. Despite all her efforts, her son's cancer spread unremittingly. Every time his body was scanned, the report showed that the cancer had engulfed yet another organ. Nonetheless, she never slowed down. She worked all through the day and hardly got any sleep at night. This went on for days, weeks, months, and years, until my nephew passed away. Even the best nurse, no matter how much you paid her, couldn't have been nearly as committed as my sister was. No want-driven person can match one who is purpose-driven, whose endeavours are unceasing even in the face of adversity.

The Want-Driven Seek External Validation, While the Purpose-Driven Don't Feel That Need

Another consequence of a lack of inner fulfilment and meaning is a need for external validation. The dissatisfied American soldiers in Vietnam looked towards their homeland for validation of their war efforts. But to their dismay, anti-war protesters were on the rise back home, further diminishing the troops' already low morale.

The Vietcong, being purpose-driven, needed no external validation. They measured their actions against the purpose they stood for. Their camp commander had said to the captive French reporter, "They have told you at Saigon that we are bandits. That is not true. We are Vietcong—Communists." The leader was proud of the role he was playing. And so were his subordinates, who shared the same clarity of purpose.

This inner motivation of the purpose-driven is further illustrated by a fable often quoted in self-help circles. Once a passerby spotted a man picking up starfish off the seashore and throwing them back into the sea. A high tide had stranded the creatures on land, and if not returned to the waters, they were destined to die within hours. The passerby appreciated the man's compassion for the dying starfish but couldn't help noticing that there were tens of thousands of them on the shore. "Given all your noble intentions, all you can do is save just a fraction of these sea stars. What difference will your efforts make?" the passerby challenged. The man didn't respond at first. Instead, he picked up another starfish and threw it back into the sea. As the creature splashed into the waters, the man pointed in that direction and replied, "I made a difference to that sea star's life."

Because he was truly driven by a sense of purpose—to save the lives of as many sea stars as he could—he couldn't have cared less about people judging the success of his endeavour. He sought no external validation for his action.

Returning to 94 Bowery, the anti-war proponents there are justified in their anti-war sentiments, but they have failed to grasp that while America's intervention in Vietnam is want-driven, Sri Krishna's objective had been to coax Arjuna into a purpose-driven battle. When Arjuna proposed to opt out of the war, viewing it as want-driven, Sri Krishna argued in favour of fighting it, but with a purpose-driven attitude:

> If a sincere person begins his journey towards karma yoga, aiming to perform his prescribed duties with a purpose-driven attitude, that's a far better option. (Bhagavad Gita 3.7)

So the swami isn't pro-war per se, but he is in favour of the purpose-driven war that Sri Krishna wanted Arjuna to fight. In fact, the swami himself is waging a purposeful life. Having come from India, alone and virtually penniless, he is trying to reach out to people with the message of the Bhagavad Gita, which he deeply believes is the panacea for all of their life's problems. Michael Grant, one of the swami's audience, jotted down later in his memoir published in 2011:

> I took stock of all I had seen and heard that evening. I couldn't really make out what the Swami was getting at when he spoke, but his strident tone—his urgency—convinced me that he had something important to say... And his humble surroundings intrigued me. Unlike the other "spiritual" people I'd met so far, the Swami obviously wasn't after pursuing his share of wealth or followers or the American dream...
>
> I added it all up, trying to fit together the pieces of this unusual puzzle—his tone, his scholarly appearance, his age, his surroundings.
>
> "He's got to be here for some sort of mission," I thought. "Why else would he speak the way he does? Why else would someone his age choose to come here of all places?"

Being Purpose-Driven Increases Your Chances of Success

A purpose-driven mindset, because it is fulfilling, empowering, and inspiring, increases your chances of success in your endeavours. It's this attitude that eventually catalysed the victory of Vietnam, a military-dwarf, over the United States, a military-giant; it enabled Arjuna to ultimately win the war of Kurukshetra against all odds; and it empowered the swami at Bowery—A. C. Bhaktivedanta Swami Prabhupada—to establish a global spiritual organisation with millions of followers, the International Society for Krishna Consciousness.

All said, understanding the benefits of a purpose-driven life is one thing, but to live it is where the challenge lies. We may have that experience of starting a task or a project on a noble note, with a selfless intent; but with time, selfishness seeps in insidiously, and we start expecting returns—some form of gratification either for the senses or the mind. Or else, our experience could be of stretching ourselves to be selfless, and then ending up with regrets for having gone too far.

The habit of being want-driven is so deeply rooted! To replace it with the habit of being purpose-driven is going to be neither easy nor quick—as with any other habit change. And that's why Sri Krishna will reveal to Arjuna a process of gradual transformation.

5

EVOLVING FROM BEING WANT-DRIVEN TO BEING PURPOSE-DRIVEN
Through Yajnas

In 2008, at a Silicon Valley conference, Google co-founder Larry Page revealed how he assesses projects: "I now have a very simple metric I use: Are you working on something that can change the world? Yes or no? The answer for 99.99999% of people is 'no'. I think we need to be training people on how to change the world."

His suggestion—that people should be trained to change the world—is a cliché. Inspirational talks promoting a purposeful lifestyle are now commonplace. But this wasn't the case a few decades ago. I believe Steven Covey was the first who alluded to the idea of being purpose-driven in 1989 when he wrote about "character ethic" in his *7 Habits of Highly Effective People*. Simon Sinek furthered the concept in his 2009 book *Start With Why*. Or perhaps it was Tony Robbins, who popularised it by calling himself the "Why Man". Regardless, it's only the Gita that has been expounding it breathlessly for thousands of years. Not only does this ancient classic exhort a purpose-driven life, but it also outlines an action plan that primes you for that kind of lifestyle.

For most modern individuals, finding a meaningful life—if at all they find it—is accidental. A classic example is Mark Bustos, a hairstylist. He made his way up in the industry until he was working at a top hair salon in New York City, earning a handsome amount. "I still didn't feel successful, so I took a step back," said Mark in an interview. Taking a break, he visited his family in the Philippines. Moved by the poverty in that country, he rented a chair in a barber's shop to give homeless orphans free haircuts. "I knew I would do something good for them," recalls Mark, "but what happened to me is something I couldn't have imagined. I realised how powerful and special what I do for a living is, and my job as a hairstylist is simply to make people happy no matter who they are. My job is to make you feel better than you did when you first sat in my chair."

Even after returning to New York City, he continued his free-haircut charity for the homeless. Every Sunday he goes out into the streets looking for people who badly need a hairstylist, and once their hair is done, he savours seeing them looking into the mirror—all smiles. In Mark's own words, "I totally found my purpose and discovered what success really means."

Mark found a meaning in life through a stroke of serendipity. But you can proactively mould your life to be purpose-driven too, says the Bhagavad Gita. And that is through Yajnas.

Yajnas, to Begin with, Cater to the Want-Driven

The word *yajna* conjures up visuals of a fire sacrifice, but the significance of this Sanskrit word goes much deeper. Yajna is about sacrificing anything that you consider valuable for something more worthy, and in the Vedas, the ubiquitously recommended method for such sacrifices happens to be through oblations made in fire seeking benedictions from the devas, the gods. But there are many fire-free yajnas too. For example, sacrificing money in philanthropy for fame or piety is called *dravyamaya yajna*, sacrificing the comforts of life for better comforts in the afterlife is *tapomaya yajna*, and sacrificing time for studying the Vedas and the Upanishads for acquiring knowledge is *svaadhyaya yajna*.

Yajnas are all-pervasive in a Vedic lifestyle and form its very fabric. They are recommended even for meeting basic needs, but most often for fulfilling varied wants. And ironically—and paradoxically—only a tiny section of the Vedic literature directly champions yajnas that are purpose-driven. And that's because, being realistic, the Vedas acknowledge that to be want-driven is the default setting of most people. Perhaps even yours!

Now, that might be embarrassing. But burying your head in the sand is never the way out, warns the Bhagavad Gita.

> One who restrains the senses of action but whose mind dwells on wants certainly deludes oneself and is called a pretender. (Bhagavad Gita 3.6)

If your mind is obsessed with desires, the Gita recommends that you fulfil them the Vedic way. By working efficiently at your workplace, while simultaneously carving out from your daily life a sacred space for yajna performances.

> Perform your prescribed duty, for doing so is better than not working. One cannot even maintain one's physical body without work. (Bhagavad Gita 3.8)

> The devas, being pleased by yajnas, will also please you, and thus, by cooperation between humans and the devas, prosperity will reign for all. (Bhagavad Gita 3.11)

Yajnas Eventually Make You Purpose-Driven

Yajna performances are a science. While they help fulfil your selfish cravings, they also smoke out the selfless attitude hidden within you—as paradoxical as that may sound. Over time, as you perform various yajnas, unbeknownst to you, you transition from being selfish to being selfless, from being apathetic to being empathetic.

That's how in ancient India, the yajna-studded Vedic traditions organically nurtured an empathetic society. With time, however, the traditions fizzled out; but the values that they imbibed got carried forward through family culture—though tapering off with every passing generation all the same. The remnants of the selfless attitude that the Vedic traditions once fostered are still visible—in traces—in rural and semi-urban India. That's why the Taj Group of Hotels, well-known for their hospitality and culture of service, scout those parts of the country for job recruitments.

The Taj Group's singular recruitment style came into the spotlight after the infamous terrorist attack on their Taj

Mahal Palace hotel in Mumbai on November 26, 2008. The extraordinary selfless manner in which the hotel employees responded received wide acclaim. The *Harvard Business Review* noted:

> Restaurant and banquet staff rushed people to safe locations such as kitchens and basements. Telephone operators stayed at their posts, alerting guests to lock doors and not step out. Kitchen staff formed human shields to protect guests during evacuation attempts. As many as 11 Taj Mumbai employees—a third of the hotel's casualties—laid down their lives while helping between 1,200 and 1,500 guests escape.

Though the Taj's training program for customer-centric care can't be undermined, their policy of enrolling candidates from places where people naturally have a service attitude has been as important according to the *Review*.

The *Review* goes on to say that the Taj Group prefers to go into the hinterland because that's where traditional Indian values—such as respect for elders and teachers, humility, consideration of others, discipline, and honesty—still hold sway. In the cities, by contrast, youngsters are increasingly driven by money, are happy to cut corners, and are unlikely to be loyal to the company or empathetic with customers.

The traditional Indian values that the *Harvard Business Review* enlisted—respect for elders and so on—were also traits brought forth by yajnas in a Vedic society, and carried forth across generations through family culture. However, the crest jewel of values those frontline workers at the Taj inherited from their forefathers was the spirit of selfless sacrifice; that was apparent in the way they risked and sacrificed their lives on the night of 26/11.

How Yajnas Change Your Habit from Being Want-Driven to Being Purpose-Driven

As we just discussed, yajnas have the potential to capsize the habit of an entire civilisation—from being want-driven to being purpose-driven—and the ripples of that transformation can be felt even generations later. To understand how yajnas bring about this habit change, we first need to know what drives a habit.

In his book *Atomic Habits*, James Clear defines a habit as "a behaviour that has been repeated enough times to become automatic." Interestingly, only those behaviours that are rewarding does the mind make automatic. The brain is like a pleasure-seeking machine that tends to rut all processes of obtaining rewards. For instance, you might be habituated to exercising daily; that's because you are reaping the benefits of including workouts in your everyday routine.

But, you may ask, what explains habits that aren't rewarding? For instance, binge-watching YouTube videos; or the habit of wasting hours scrolling down the Instagram feed. You may feel terrible towards the end of these activities, having lost productive time. How is it that such punishing behaviours have been made automatic by the mind? That's because these activities have rewarded you in the past—and to such an extent that your mind has developed a craving for those pleasures that you once derived. So even though those rewards have now died, that craving keeps the mind's hopes alive, thus keeping the habit intact. In essence, cravings are the driving force behind every habit.

Yajnas modify the mind's craving, thus catalysing a habit change. I have observed this first hand; I have witnessed the alteration of consciousness of my own parents. Coming from a traditional, rural South Indian family, all through my childhood I saw them perform fire yajnas every now and then. And as was the ritual, the ceremony always ended with a spread served out to every guest, and gifts given out after the feast. Charities were as integral to the function as were oblations offered into the sacrificial pit. Though all that expenditure was with the expectation of some return—either to meet a need or to fulfil a want—my mum and dad always turned to yajnas for the rewards they sought. In other words, instead of solely resorting to the go-grab approach that's characteristic of we moderns, they believed in the ancient wisdom that giving away was indispensable even for material well-being. And I surmise that this Vedic formula, though counterintuitive, did reward them with whatever they wanted. For, their enthusiasm for conducting these rituals was unabating—was in fact soaring—as they performed them year after year.

My father is now 82 years old, and my mother 73. Recently they performed a major yajna, which they feel would probably be the last big one of their lives. They believe they won't live long enough to do another one. Though their contemplation on dying was deeply saddening, what was impressive was their intent behind performing this ceremony. They did it solely for the opportunity to invite the villagers, feed them sumptuously and give away gifts profusely—to the extent of exhausting their entire life's savings. And this time they were expecting nothing in return.

The yajnas they had performed over the decades had finally borne the Holy Grail—the attitude of selflessness. From being want-driven, they were finally purpose-driven.

The acts of selfless sacrifice and service that are woven into the rituals or procedures of a yajna release a quantum of spiritual happiness that the soul longs to relish. So every time we perform a yajna, non-consciously we experience a little of that inner joy, even though our conscious intent for performing the ceremony may be selfish. That higher spiritual happiness accumulates with every yajna performed until the craving for that inner reward of selfless joy surpasses the external reward of selfish pleasure. And with that change in craving, the habit too changes from being want-driven to being purpose-driven.

My parents might have performed just a fraction of the yajnas recommended in the Vedas, and that itself proved quite effective in catalysing a substantial change within a lifetime. Obviously, if the Vedic culture is embraced in its entirety, the transformation will be much quicker.

"Well, yajnas paving the way for a purpose-driven life makes sense," you might muse. "But the elaborate rituals that shroud them seem superstitious. Why not pare out those fire ceremonies, chanting of hymns and so on, and just stick to what seems to be the essence, that is philanthropy and charity?" That's a good question, and for an answer, we first need to understand the subtle obstacles we may face on our journey towards being purpose-driven.

6

HURDLES ON THE WAY TO A PURPOSE-DRIVEN LIFE
Controllership and Doership

On October 5, 2011, the world lost a legend. He was for information technology what Henry Ford was for automobiles. He had the grit of Edison, and an uncanny brilliance unparalleled even in the pantheon of the all-time greats. He was Steve Jobs. Had cancer not ripped through his body at the unripe age of 56, the way we live would continue to change in ways wildly unfathomable.

Right in the introduction of Jobs' biography, however, biographer Walter Isaacson cautions the reader—"He (Jobs) was not a model boss or human being, tidily packaged for emulation." Ironically, the lead-ups to the ending of Jobs' life story leave us with the same stern reminder.

The Problem with Being a Control Freak

In October 2003 when the tumour in Jobs' pancreas was first seen, his doctors effused over the early detection; they said it could be surgically removed before it had definitively spread. But Jobs decided to evade the surgery—which was the only accepted medical approach—and betted instead on a weird assortment of alternative therapies. His wife, friends, and doctors tried to persuade him to get operated on, but he was obstinate. "He has that ability to ignore stuff he doesn't want to confront," his wife Powell later explained. Art Levinson, who was on the Apple board and concurrently ran a firm that made cancer treatment drugs, was also among those who vainly tried to bring Jobs around. Levinson later said in retrospect, "I think Steve has such a strong desire for the world to be a certain way that he wills it to be that way. Sometimes it doesn't work. Reality is unforgiving." After nine months, the tumour had grown to an unignorable proportion. Only then did Jobs agree to the surgery. But the cancer had already made its irrepressible headway; the unforgiving reality had punished him for defying it for so long.

The main problem with Jobs was that he preferred to live in a world that revolved with him as its centre, a world where he was in control. Anything outside of that he ignored, whether the issue was personal or professional. That's how he burnt people around him, both at home and at the office. His eldest daughter Lisa vented out her hurt in her memoir *Small Fry*. "He was starting this rocket-ship career and I don't imagine I fit into that so well," she said to the press after the book release, as if explaining the instances when she felt ignored by her father. And at the office, Jobs sidelined people by similar parameters. "I think that he likes people to jump when he says jump... He doesn't seem to like people who see him without a halo," said Jeff Raskin, one of his colleagues. Raskin wasn't the kind who followed Jobs' commands. So Jobs adopted Raskin's baby project, the Macintosh, and got Raskin ousted. For the Macintosh, the change of leadership turned out just as well. Nonetheless, on Raskin it was an injustice that was inflicted.

The Problem with Doership

Doership naturally follows controllership. Therefore, in the world Jobs had built for himself, he yearned to be the only doer, the sole go-getter. That's how, with no qualms, he claimed the ideas of others as his own. Again, it was Raskin who pointed this out: "Very often, when told of a new idea, he will immediately attack it and say it is worthless or even stupid... but if the idea is a good one, he will soon be telling people about it as though it was his own." Raskin wasn't the only one to make this observation. Jonathan Ive, one of Jobs' closest aides and companions, had something similar to say about Jobs: "He will go through a process of looking at my idea and say, 'That's no good. That's not very good. I like that one.' And later I will be sitting in the audience and he will be talking about it as if it was his idea." Ive felt this attitude of Jobs made Apple vulnerable as a company, and Ive's thoughts resonate with what Jim Collins says in his bestseller *Good to Great*.

A book based on extensive research, *Good to Great* is all about the kind of leadership required to make a company great. Collins calls such a leader a Level Five executive. Among other things—like humility and strong professional will—a distinguishing factor of such a leader is that he or she gives credit to others in the face of success, and takes the blame in the disgrace of failure. In other words, a Level Five executive is more or less the antithesis of Steve Jobs! "But didn't Jobs make Apple great?"—Jobs' fans may bristle. Yes, he did, except that our conception of greatness may not match with Collins' definition. One important criterion of a great company, as Collins defines it, is that it's "built to last". So, Apple's greatness should be judged more by how well it fared after Jobs' departure, than by its accomplishments while he was alive. Again, we could be in for a debate here. Some say Apple died with Steve Jobs; others claim it's alive and thriving. A definitive answer only time will tell. But one thing can perhaps be unanimously agreed upon: if it were not for Jobs' obsession with controllership and doership, he definitely would have left behind a better legacy. Substantiating this is Isaacson's remark in Jobs' biography, "...he (Jobs) had never truly empowered a deputy or shared the stage." This again is the antithesis of what makes for a Level Five leader, who prioritises grooming a successor. Whatever Apple is after Jobs' departure, the credit perhaps goes more to Tim Cook, Jobs' successor, than to Jobs himself. Without any formal training from Jobs, he took on the reins of Apple at short notice, initially when Jobs fell sick, and later after Jobs passed away.

Jobs' hunger for doership didn't spare even Steve Wozniak, his friend and co-founder of Apple who catapulted the company to glory with the development of the Apple II. Though Jobs had a considerable say in the computer's success, it was chiefly a Wozniak product—and Jobs acknowledged that silently. But then he was desperate for a product he could claim to be his own. Thus, he went on a tangent and eventually hijacked the Macintosh project. Once that happened, he ensured the company doted on the Macintosh—a product still under development—and downplayed the Apple II—the product that brought in most revenues. Even Wozniak, who was otherwise sweet-natured, was livid. He decided to quit Apple.

In 1985, when Steve Jobs was given the boot by the Apple board, he played the victim card. But in reality, it was karma boomeranging. He had caused his own undoing by pushing his controllership and doership to the limits. Were it not for his other-worldly genius, his charisma, the abating of his controlling tendencies in the years to come, and a lot of good luck, he could never have made a comeback in 1997 and become a legend of innovation. His story would have prematurely ended like the tale of most control freaks.

A classic example of such a tragic end is that of John DeLorean's career. The founder of DeLorean Motor Company, he shared many parallels with Steve Jobs. Both had a keen eye for revolutionary design, both loved the intersection of aesthetics and technology, both loved to belittle their competitors, both were superlatively driven, and most of all—both were plagued by controllership and doership. Except that DeLorean didn't bounce back after his ego brought him down. Another example is that of Edwin Land, the co-founder of Polaroid Corporation who was also ousted from his company for being a control freak—and never made a comeback. But fortunately for him, he enjoyed a lot of success before the dark side of him catalysed his downfall.

Author Ryan Holiday, who is considered one of the finest thinkers of our times, confronts the puzzle of Jobs' success despite being driven by demons. "...what we see when we study these people is that they did their best work in the moments when they fought back against these impulses, disorders, and flaws," he says, and he's spot on. Before the scheduled launch of Apple Stores, for instance, Jobs ceded control to pay heed to someone else's advice, the event was rescheduled to incorporate the new inputs, and that's how the project turned out successful.

Following Jobs' example without filtering out his shortcomings from his strengths—or worse—mistaking his shortcomings to be his strengths, could lead us into deep waters. As it happened with Elizabeth Holmes, the infamous CEO of the now-defunct company Theranos. She emulated Jobs in toto, to the extent of wearing a black turtleneck at the workplace, like Jobs did.

Controllership and Doership Drag You Back to Being Want-Driven

All that said, the worst underside of controllership and doership we haven't discussed yet. And here it is: these tendencies drive a craving that could be deeper than that experienced through gross external rewards. Take, for example, the simple—yet addictive—mobile game of Tetris. It's a block-puzzle game with blocks of varied shapes randomly dropping in from the top of the screen. By adjusting their orientation and position through tapping and swiping on the screen, the player has to put them in order before they reach the bottom; the idea is to build perfect lines as the blocks pile up below. Every time you form a line, you experience the kick—"I did it!" Tetris has been extant since the 1980s and is still popular. Only the devices it's played on have kept evolving. As I travel through the local trains in Mumbai, I often see passengers immersed either in Tetris or some improvisation of it like the Candy Crush Saga. I am unsure if those who play it broadcast their scores for laurels; that would be risible. Controlling the blocks and doing perfect lines is their only reward. And they crave exactly that.

The craving to be the controller and doer is a self-centred one. And as long as we are under its sway, it's hard to be authentically purpose-driven, for a purposeful life—at its core—is all about being selfless. On the surface we may be philanthropic, charitable or purpose-driven, but our heart will remain vacant if we pride ourselves on being doers of good to others. And as long as there's no inner fulfilment, we remain want-driven—if not overtly, then covertly.

Even Steve Jobs spoke about "putting things back into the stream of history and of human consciousness", but his controllership and doership held him firmly captive in the camp of the want-driven. That was evident from the way he struggled to let go all through his life. His success streak was interspersed by long stretches of insecurity, stress, anxiety, anger, and arrogance that accompany the tendency to hold on beyond limits. Put plainly—his less than happy life of selfishness was peppered with successes. It could be hard to digest what I just said. But we need to overcome the human tendency of focusing on and replicating the proverbial greener grass in the lives of celebrities. Paying equal heed to the vast terrain of the not-so-green can teach us what not to copy from their story, and that's as important.

Continuing on our discussion of yajnas from the previous chapter, the spirit of these procedures and the rituals that surround them are designed to not just help overcome the gross craving for external rewards, but also the subtle craving to be the doer and the controller. Yajnas are an elaborate science which we shall be dissecting further.

7

UNLEASHING THE POWER OF DEPENDENCY
Through Rituals

"I'm probably just talking to a tree right now. But if you're there, I need to give you a heads-up," whispers the protagonist Jake Sully as he religiously kneels in front of the deity of Planet Pandora—the Tree of Souls. Jake is an immigrant from Planet Earth and is now leading the natives of Pandora in their fightback against invaders from the very planet he hails from. Humans, eyeing this newly discovered planet's rich natural resources, are poised to take over. "See the world we come from," Jake continues his prayer, "There's no green there. They killed their Mother (nature). And they're gonna do the same here. More Sky People (humans) are gonna come. They're gonna come like a rain that never ends. Unless we stop them... I will stand and fight. You know I will. But I need a little help here."

For those who missed watching *Avatar*, the Hollywood sci-fi movie from 2009, what I just described was a scene from that blockbuster. When adjusted for inflation, the film is the second highest-grossing of all time. Most movie buffs chalk up the movie's astronomical success to its visual effects, especially to the epochal 3D tech. But film punditry also alludes that *Avatar's* famed filmmaker James Cameron, who has routinely proved film critics wrong, perhaps knows better. According to him, the film shot to No. 1 in every market across the globe because it dealt with universal truths of the "human condition that transcends culture."

The Power of Dependency

Depending on higher powers for success in one's endeavours is one such universal truth of the human condition, and Cameron depicts that deftly in the afore-described scene from *Avatar*. Our ancestors, both from the East and the West, embraced this dependency, which is the antithesis of controllership and doership. "And then the Renaissance came and everything changed, and we had this big idea, and the big idea was, let's put the individual human being at the centre of the universe above all gods and mysteries," notes journalist and author Elizabeth Gilbert. "It just completely warps and distorts egos, and it creates all these unmanageable expectations about performance."

"You know, in the Middle Ages, in England, when you met a very poor person, that person would be described as an 'unfortunate'—literally, somebody who had not been blessed by fortune, an unfortunate. Nowadays, particularly in the United States, if you meet someone at the bottom of society, they may unkindly be described as a 'loser.' There's a real difference between an unfortunate and a loser, and that shows 400 years of evolution in society and our belief in who is responsible for our lives. It's no longer the gods, it's us. We're in the driving seat," observes the British philosopher Alain de Botton.

This paradigm shift—from dependency to controllership—has bred volatility in our society's psyche. While our ancestors remained equanimous both in success and failure, we moderns are prone to be arrogant in the face of success, depressed in the disgrace of failure, and stressed out all the while. We are overburdened by a disproportionate sense of responsibility towards the outcome.

Nevertheless, most of us continue to view dependency as a weakness.

Recently, though, I happened upon a story that rebutted that perspective. A little girl and her father were walking through the woods when they came across a fallen tree blocking their path. "Do you think I can move that tree if I try?" the girl asked. "If you use all your strength, you can," replied the father. The girl gave it her best shot but failed. "You got it wrong, Dad. I couldn't do it," she said with an impish smile. "Try again with all your strength," retorted the father. She tried once more and again she failed. "I can't do it," she resigned. But the father stood firm, "I advised you to use all your strength. But you didn't ask for my help!"

"When every hope is gone, 'when helpers fail and comforts flee,' I find that help arrives somehow, from I know not where. Supplication, worship, prayer are no superstition;

they are acts more real than the acts of eating, drinking, sitting, or walking. It is no exaggeration to say that they alone are real, all else is unreal," said Mahatma Gandhi. Inspired by Gandhi, Martin Luther King prayed, "God, give us strength of body to keep walking for freedom. God, give us strength to remain nonviolent, even though we may face death." Their attitude of dependence on God empowered them to achieve the seemingly impossible.

Interestingly, the fourth most popular TED Talk of all time is titled "The Power of Vulnerability." In it, professor and researcher Brené Brown explains how vulnerability—a state in which you realise how little control you have and how little you can do to change a given situation—is the "birthplace of joy". Because that's when you understand that all you can do is try your very best and depend on the gods for the rest, an aha moment that lifts tons of burden off you, allowing you to freely enjoy the work you are doing to the fullest.

Creativity and Dependency

Dependency on higher powers can also make you grittier. Even if you fail time and time again, you aren't afraid to keep trying. You understand that all you can do is your best; the rest is beyond your control anyway; the gods take the fall, if at all you continue to fail.

Grit, in turn, is the birthplace of creativity, because creativity ceases the moment you stop trying. That's why Julia Cameron, the author of the legendary *The Artist's Way*, prods creatives to thumb their nose at the tendency towards controllership, saying, "Leap, and (then) the net will appear." In other words, it's the urge to control the outcome that prevents us from "leaping"—from giving fresh ideas a spirited try. And unless we keep trying, we remain unlikely to stumble upon something that resonates. "The odds of producing an influential or successful idea are a positive function of the total number of ideas generated," confirms psychologist Dean Simonton, as quoted by author Adam Grant in *Originals*.

To add it all up, dependency is cardinal for both a joyful and creative life.

And yajnas are instrumental in training you in that art. The rituals, the hymns, and every other nuance of a Vedic sacrifice are designed to impress upon your subconscious mind your state of dependency.

To curb the conscious mind, the Gita provides reasons for performing yajnas, all of which point to the same inherent position of dependency of the soul.

> In the beginning of creation, the one Supreme Lord sent forth generations of beings, along with yajnas, and blessed them by saying, "Be thou happy by this yajna because its performance will bestow upon you everything desirable for both your wants and your needs." (Bhagavad Gita 3.10)

> The demigods, being pleased by yajnas, will also please you, and thus, by cooperation between humans and the demigods, prosperity will reign for all. (Bhagavad Gita 3.11)

> In charge of the various necessities of life, the demigods, being satisfied by the performance of yajna, will supply all necessities to you. But one who enjoys such gifts without

offering them to the demigods in return is certainly a thief. (Bhagavad Gita 3.12)

One who does not follow in human life the cycle of sacrifice thus established by the Vedas certainly leads a life steeped in ingratitude. Living only for the satisfaction of the senses, such a person lives in vain. (Bhagavad Gita 3.16)

Thus, through the allure of prosperity, the threat of punishment, and the inspiration of gratitude for the demigods—by some means or other—the Gita encourages you to perform yajnas. Because, that's how you can cultivate selflessness, relinquish controllership, and consequently develop a purpose-driven attitude towards life.

But are these demigods a fiction invented by our patriarchs to rein in the human ego, or do they genuinely exist?

In *Avatar* at least, the demigod to whom Jake prays is depicted as real. During the fight that ensues, when the army of the natives led by Jake is on the brink of defeat, a miracle occurs: the beasts and birds of Pandora ally with the natives to turn the tide against the invaders. Neytiri, the fierce warrior from Pandora who is also Jake's love interest, is elated and shouts out to Jake that his prayers have been answered.

Real life, however, is different from the spectacle of the silver screen. Rather than seeking validation of belief in the demigods from Hollywood, Bollywood, or sentimentalism, we perhaps should turn to modern science.

Or... should we?

8

RELYING ON TRUST IS UNAVOIDABLE
Whether in Material Life or Spiritual Life

In 2011, an experiment conducted at the inconspicuous Utrecht train station in the Netherlands gained significant attention. Diederik Stapel, a professor at the University of Tilburg and an academic star in the field of human attitudes and behaviours, had designed the study. Among the rows of chairs in the train station, the first chair of each row was occupied by either a white volunteer or a black one. Subsequently, white passengers who were waiting for their trains were invited to come over and occupy one of the other chairs in order to fill out a questionnaire. Researchers observed that the white passengers tended to sit farther from the black passengers on days when the surrounding area was strewn with rubbish. It was a stark finding that demonstrated how an unclean environment brought out racist tendencies in individuals—a concern for countries grappling with racism.

Placing Trust in Academia

Experiments in psychology and social psychology, like the one quoted above, form the staple of self-help books today. They offer insight into how we can improve our personal lives and better our homes, workplaces, and society. We are inspired to implement these revelations, placing our trust in them wholeheartedly. After all, we surmise, these findings are scientifically validated through rational empiricism: observed by the senses and reasoned out by the intellect.

In the aforementioned study, for example, the passengers were *observed* occupying different seats, the trash was *observed* whenever present, and the two observations were *rationally* correlated to draw an inference. Perfect and flawless methodology! Except that the entire experiment was fabricated. It was never conducted; rather, it was concocted for an academic journal by Diederik Stapel.

I highlight a fabricated experiment not to undermine science or the scientific method, but to spotlight a reality often overlooked by most scientific minds—that when it comes to knowledge acquisition, we often have little choice but to rely on what we deem reliable or reputed sources, rather than on rational or empirical data that we have gathered or verified ourselves. It's simply impractical to personally verify even a fraction of the plethora of information—scientific or otherwise—that we encounter in everyday life. Therefore, in science, spirituality, or any other field, the bottom line is the trust we place in the source of information.

In primary school, for instance, I was a novice in science, and was taught about atomic structure. The textbooks told me of Rutherford's gold foil experiment, Thomson's study with cathode ray tubes, and so on. If I were an orthodox rational empiricist, I would have had to replicate those experiments, observe the results and verify the conclusions, all on my own. The downside? At this ripe age of 43, I'd likely still be mired in primary school. Fortunately, I placed my trust in the school textbooks and graduated on time. The credit perhaps goes more to my teachers, who had instilled in me the notion that trusting modern science and school textbooks was risk-free. Even though their guidance turned out well, what they had imprinted on my impressionable mind was more a figment than a fact. Modern science, too, has its pitfalls.

In 2013, *The New York Times* ran an article on Diederik Stapel's deception, "The Mind of a Con Man," authored by Yudhijit Bhattacharjee. "Each case of research fraud that's uncovered triggers a similar response from scientists. First disbelief, then anger, then a tendency to dismiss the perpetrator as one rotten egg in an otherwise-honest enterprise. But the scientific misconduct that has come to light in recent years suggests at the very least that the number of bad actors in science isn't as insignificant as many would like to believe," writes Bhattacharjee in the article. He goes on to quote Stapel: "People think of scientists as monks in a monastery looking out for the truth. People have lost faith in the church, but they haven't lost faith in science. My behaviour shows that science is not holy. There are scarce resources, you need grants, you need money, there is competition. Normal people go to the edge to get that money. Science is of course about discovery, about digging to discover the truth. But it is also communication, persuasion, marketing. I am a salesman. I am on the road. People are on the road with their talk. With the same talk. It's like a circus." In other words, academic science too has turned into a business seeking funding rather than stark truth.

Stapel committed fraud in at least 55 of his papers, as well as in 10 Ph.D. dissertations written by his students. This extent of deception is surely over the top and can be considered a rarity. However, the "misuse of statistics, ignoring of data that do not conform to a desired hypothesis and the pursuit of a compelling story no matter how scientifically unsupported it may be" are now commonplace practices in academic circles, according to *The New York Times* article.

I don't mean to drag modern science through the mud. After all, so much of our lifestyle is dependent on it. At the end of the day, all of us—myself included—will have to continue to trust this progressive branch of knowledge and its torchbearers. We have little choice here—and that's precisely my point. Let's learn to acknowledge that much of our life is based on trusting something that isn't foolproof.

Placing Trust in the Media

A word is in order here about the burgeoning media industry. Of course, fewer would bet on the veracity of what the news outlets churn out, as compared to scientific findings. But what about reputed newspapers like *The New York Times*? They are certainly considered exceptionally authoritative.

For instance, when I quoted *The New York Times* to support my point concerning deception in scientific circles, didn't that strengthen my case? Obviously, it did. However, ironically, trusting one of the most reputed newspapers on earth may not pay off all the time.

Take, for instance, the murder story of Kitty Genovese that I had earlier cited from *The New York Times*. Forty years after the assault, Kitty's brother Bill was inspired to reinvestigate the case, layer by layer. Based on his findings, he produced the documentary—*The Witness*—that was nominated for an Academy Award for Best Documentary Feature. The film scathingly exposed the media's instinct to sensationalise news items. "While there was no question that the attack occurred, and that some neighbours ignored cries for help, the portrayal of 38 witnesses as fully aware and unresponsive was erroneous. The article (on Kitty's murder published in 1964) grossly exaggerated the number of witnesses and what they had perceived. None saw the attack in its entirety. Only a few had glimpsed parts of it or recognised the cries for help. Many thought they had heard lovers or drunks quarrelling. There were two attacks, not three. And afterward, two people did call the police," admitted *The New York Times* in a write-up published in 2016, following the documentary's release.

While *The New York Times* acknowledged its flaws in 2016, it was the BBC's turn in 2021 when an investigation sniffed out that a sensational scoop bagged by one of its journalists was through deception. Way back in 1995, journalist Martin Bashir had tricked Princess Diana into an interview that aired the British royal family's dirty linen in front of an audience of 20 million. Diana herself seemed the most affected by the repercussions, going by her son Prince William's public statement: "The BBC's failure contributed significantly to her fear, paranoia, and isolation that I remember from those final years with her."

"The worst and most serious aspect of it (the deception scandal) was the cover-up," admitted Lord Grade, former chairman of the broadcasting corporation. He was referring to the clean chit given to the "rogue reporter" by the BBC's own investigation team when accusations of foul play had surfaced immediately after the interview was aired in 1995. "The BBC believes that if you own up to your mistakes early on, it's a sign of weakness... It's a cultural flaw deep in the heart of BBC journalism," added the former chairman ruefully.

With its reputation hanging by a thread, the BBC issued an unconditional apology: "The process for securing the interview fell far short of what audiences have a right to expect. The BBC should have made a greater effort to get to the bottom of what happened at the time and been more transparent about what it knew. While the BBC cannot turn back the clock after a quarter of a century, we can make a full and unconditional apology. The BBC offers that today." Finally, after 25 years! Nonetheless, better late than never.

To sum it all up, underpinning much of our life is the trust that we invest in what we count as authoritative or reliable sources of information. Nonetheless, we get betrayed at times, either by modern science, the media, or any other source we believe in. And yet, we have little choice but to remain faithful. Or else, life will come to a grinding halt.

The Role of Trust in Spiritual Life

As in material life, so also in the spiritual. Not all information in the Bhagavad Gita can be verified by the senses or reasoned out by the intellect, especially when we are beginners. But we have little choice other than to place our faith in this authoritative Vedic literature which has stood the test of time. Else, spiritual life remains a non-starter. And yes, if you feel dubious over trusting the Gita, just remind yourself that there are hardly any risk-free trust-based investments in life. Only that you are betting on something spiritual this time, something you may not have tried before, something that isn't considered cool. That's why the mind is freaking out. Just give these feelings a cold shoulder, and soldier on.

So, yes. The Bhagavad Gita indicates that we should trust that the demigods, higher beings empowered by God, are for real; only that we can't perceive them with our present state of consciousness. If you think about it, it makes sense to believe in their existence. As it took several geniuses to notch up the propeller speed of an aircraft to 1,500 revolutions per minute, it's believable that some unearthly brilliance enabled a hummingbird to flap its wings 80 times in a second which is 4,800 times per minute, roughly three times faster than an aircraft propeller. As it takes the experience of a civil engineer to construct a functioning water tank, it's logical that it was the expertise of a cosmic engineer that created clouds—vessels that hold gallons of water, yet so light that they float in the sky, and so sparse that an airplane can pass by.

According to the Vedas, it's these demigods who run the universe. As there are people responsible for supplying water to the city, so also the demigod Varuna provides water at the level of the cosmos. As there are people to light up our homes, so also the demigods Vivasvan and Soma illuminate the world through sunlight and moonlight. As there are corporations producing well-designed, smoothly functioning products, so also do the demigods cooperatively create a well-rounded and smoothly functioning cosmos with beautiful flowers, delicious fruits, graceful birds, majestic animals, and a symbiosis that ties them all into one self-sustaining unit.

9

THE PURPOSE-DRIVEN VIS-À-VIS THE RESPONSIBILITY-DRIVEN
Their Similarities and Differences

On June 6, 1944—often referred to as D-Day—Allied forces launched the largest seaborne invasion in history with the objective of reclaiming France from the Nazis. During the operation, American soldiers landing on Omaha Beach suffered heavy losses while assaulting fortified German defensive positions. Captain John H. Miller lost 35 men of his battalion—and that included Sean Ryan.

Sean Ryan's brother, Peter Ryan, was killed in action at Utah on the same day, and their brother Daniel Ryan had died in combat at New Guinea a week before. The news of the three brothers' death was relayed to Washington DC. It was now the state's responsibility to console their bereaved mother; Sir Abraham Lincoln had set the precedent a long time ago by personally penning a letter to a lady who had lost all five sons in the Civil War: "I feel how weak and fruitless must be any words of mine that would attempt to beguile you from the grief of a loss so overwhelming. But I cannot refrain from tendering to you the consolation that may be found in the thanks of the Republic they died to save..."

The chief of staff at Washington DC decided that something more than a letter of condolence should be sent to the mother of the Ryans. He ordered a search for James Ryan, the fourth of the brothers and the lone surviving son of the mother, to be carried out on the war field and for him to be sent back home. According to reports, James had been airdropped a day before D-Day somewhere close to Captain Miller's billet at Omaha.

The captain was wired the order to find Private James Ryan. After recruiting seven men from his company, Miller set out on this unusual mission: searching for a private in war-ridden France was like looking for a needle in a stack of needles. Besides, was it worth venturing eight soldiers into a swarm of German reinforcements for the sake of one private? Despite these misgivings, the party was undeterred in their search because of a sense of responsibility they bore. They lost two men to German snipers during the search, but finally found Ryan, who was babysitting a key bridge along with a small group of paratroopers. Ryan was informed of the death of his brothers and was asked to leave, but he was adamant about staying. He felt duty-bound to deter the Germans from crossing the bridge at all costs.

Miller and his party were committed to taking Ryan back to his mother. They, too, decided to wait until the enemies were detained, meanwhile sharing Ryan's responsibility of guarding the bridge. The Germans soon arrived with heavy ammunition, and in the fight that ensued, Miller and three more of his men were killed. However, Ryan survived and was taken home to console his mother.

This saga of responsibility that I have described in broad strokes was the plot of the 1998 blockbuster, *Saving Private Ryan*. The film, loosely based on a true story from World War II, was nominated for 11 Academy Awards, won five, and is considered one of the greatest Hollywood films of all time.

Pulitzer Prize winner Mary Schmich once said, "The movies we love and admire are to some extent a function of who we are when we see them." American film critic David Ansen echoed this relationship between moviegoers and movies when he quipped, "We are the movies and the movies are us." Put simply, we like the movies that showcase what we yearn for in real life.

Saving Private Ryan was a roaring success because we love the notion of responsibility. We want our governments to be more responsible; we dream of a more responsible society; we wish—at least at times—that we had more responsible parents; we demand our siblings to be more responsible; we prefer the company of responsible relatives and friends; we look out for a responsible life partner; we hope to beget responsible children; we pray to have a responsible boss; we screen for responsible colleagues; and we preach to subordinates to be more responsible.

But the irony of our times is that we tend to cut corners with our own responsibilities.

A Responsible World Is a Better World

The following anecdote exemplifies how the world would be a far better place if each one of us paid more attention to our own responsibility towards others rather than wasting time carping over how others are irresponsible:

There were 50 people attending a seminar. Each was handed a balloon and asked to write their name on it. The balloons were then collected and strewn about in a room nearby. "Go to the other room and find the balloon with your name on it," said the facilitator. "And do it within five minutes." The participants scurried to the other room and rummaged. None succeeded in their search, but conveniently placed the blame on the commotion in the room: if only the other participants were more sedate! The facilitator called all of them back and explained the second half of the exercise. "Again, go to the other room. But this time, responsibly deliver the first balloon that you lay your hands on to whomever it belongs to." The participants followed the instructions and returned with their respective balloons in less than two minutes. "A responsible world in which everyone focuses on one's own responsibility rather than on the irresponsibility of others can be set right in no time," exclaimed the facilitator.

The Two Sides of Irresponsibility

The tendency to oscillate between irresponsible attachment (*bhoga*) and irresponsible detachment (*tyaga*) is a hallmark of the new-age psyche. Steve Jobs serves as a perfect—though extreme—example. Laurene Powell was the second person with whom Steve Jobs became seriously involved, romantically. She was a victim of Jobs' mood swings. Laurene's close friend Kat Smith once disclosed, "Jobs has the power to focus like a laser beam, and when it came across you, you basked in the light of his affection. When it moved to another point of focus, it was very, very dark for you. It was very confusing to Laurene."

Tina Redse was the first person Jobs was "truly in love with," as he himself once said. The two were physically passionate and prone to public displays of affection. Yet, Tina was also baffled by how uncaring Jobs could be at times. "Neglect is a form of abuse," she once scrawled on the wall of the hallway to their bedroom. She seemed to have accurately diagnosed the cause behind Jobs' temperamental behaviour. "She would later recall how incredibly painful it was to be in love with someone *so* self-centred," writes Isaacson in Steve Jobs' biography.

One corollary of being self-centred is being irresponsible towards the feelings of others. Such an irresponsible person is affectionate when he feels the need for the partner, and is detached when he doesn't; the feelings of the other are never a consideration. Needless to say, an irresponsible person struggles with relationships; Jobs, however, always had the stars on his side. He was fortunate that Laurene Powell decided to marry him and adjust to his quirks.

An attitude of irresponsibility is rife even in today's workplaces. Employees quit on a whim midway through a project, and employers lay off staff midway through a financial crisis. But, as strange as it may sound, being responsible has its perks, even in a cutthroat corporate culture. A classic example is the success story of Alcoa—Aluminium Company of America—under the leadership of Paul O'Neill. In his first address to investors following his appointment as CEO in 1987, O'Neill began with the words, "I want to talk to you about worker safety... I intend to make Alcoa the safest company in America." Within a year of this unconventional speech in which he spoke nothing about profit-making, Alcoa's profits hit a record high. By the time he retired in 2000, the company's annual net income was five times larger than before he arrived. All because he introduced a culture of responsibility from the top-down that bred confidence and constancy in the workforce, which in turn automatically led to productivity and profits.

The Vedas Advocate a Responsible Attitude

The Vedas exhort us to nurture a responsible attitude in every aspect of life. We are encouraged to acknowledge that we are indebted, not just to our family for their physical and emotional care, but also to many others in society for their various services; that we are obliged, not just to the devas for running the cosmos, but also to every living entity for contributing towards a balanced ecology. And so we are expected to absolve these debts—by caring for our family, giving back to society, performing yajnas for the heavenly, and loving every living entity.

Even the Bhagavad Gita insists that we act responsibly. If Arjuna were want-driven, he should continue with his prescribed duty of fighting along with performance of yajnas;

that was Sri Krishna's recommendation, as we discussed earlier. But even if Arjuna claimed to be purpose-driven, there was no scope for him escaping his duty prematurely.

> As most people perform their duties being want-driven, you may similarly act, but being purpose-driven, for the sake of leading others on the right path. (Bhagavad Gita 3.25)
>
> Kings such as Janaka attained perfection solely by performance of prescribed duties. Therefore, just for the sake of educating the people in general, you should perform your work. (Bhagavad Gita 3.20)
>
> Whatever action a great person performs, common people follow. And whatever standards he or she sets by exemplary acts, all the world pursues. (Bhagavad Gita 3.21)
>
> O son of Pratha, there is no work prescribed for me within all the three planetary systems. Nor am I in want of anything, nor have I a need to obtain anything—and yet I am engaged in prescribed duties. (Bhagavad Gita 3.22)
>
> For if I ever failed to engage in carefully performing prescribed duties, O Partha, certainly people would follow my path. (Bhagavad Gita 3.23)

Responsibility and Purpose

Give it a second thought, and you will realise that a sense of responsibility aids in being more purpose-driven, and vice versa. Both are about being less selfish and more selfless, about having a cause bigger than oneself, and about leading a meaningful life. The only difference is that while a sense of purpose blossoms from a deeper space—the heart—a sense of responsibility relies on the reasoning of the head. While being purposeful can sometimes seem irrational, you are truly inspired to be dutiful only when it appears sensible.

For instance, in the movie *Saving Private Ryan*, the dutiful Captain Miller is seen struggling, trying to rationalise the mission he is leading. "You see," he expresses to a confidant, "when one of your men ends up being killed, you tell yourself it happened so you could save the lives of two or three or 10 others...maybe a 100 others. And that's how simple it is. That's how you rationalise making the choice between the mission and the men. Except this time, the mission is a man. This Ryan better be worth it. He'd better go home, cure some disease, or invent a longer-lasting light bulb or something. Because the truth is I wouldn't trade 10 Ryans for even one of my trained men."

Not to suggest that the Gita advises you to irrationally commit yourselves to any purpose that comes your way. We can't afford to squander the purpose-driven attitude so painstakingly earned on a purpose that's not worth the candle!

PART III

In Search of a Worthy Purpose

10

BEING PURPOSE-DRIVEN: WHAT DOES IT REALLY MEAN?
A Deeper Look

One day late in the October of 1980, a 45-year-old Australian novelist, Thomas Keneally, went shopping in Beverly Hills, seeking a modestly priced briefcase. He entered a store and struck up a conversation with its proprietor, Leopold Page, a Holocaust survivor. When Keneally mentioned he was an author, Page pricked up his ears and proclaimed, "I know a wonderful story. It is not a story for Jews but for everyone. A story of humanity, man to man... it's a story for you, Thomas. It's a story for you, I swear." Page wished that the author penned this real-life tale that had unfolded during World War II. The documents containing facts and figures underpinning the story, Page had painstakingly collected over the decades. Many of the people who were part of this legend were still alive, though scattered across continents. Page was willing to contact them and persuade them for an interview with Keneally. All that Keneally had to do was curate all this information into a smooth and engrossing narrative—and Page was confident it would be a surefire bestseller.

The story that Page wanted the world to know was that of Oskar Schindler, a Nazi agent of the German military agency, who was more preoccupied as a businessman during World War II. Want-driven and opportunistic, he went to Krakow, a Polish city invaded by the Germans, in 1939. Setting up a factory there that manufactured goods for both the war effort and the black market, he recruited labourers from the Plaszow concentration camp that sat on the northern edge of the city. Schindler was a shrewd entrepreneur who knew that productivity follows an inspired workforce: he treated his Jewish prison-labourers with kindness. They were kept safe from the whims of SS soldiers who casually toyed with shooting them down. And were well-fed, unlike prisoners in typical concentration camps. Over the years, Schindler made a fortune for sure, and in the process, also earned something he never aimed for—the gratitude of his prisoners. They felt safe and cared for in Schindler's haven, amid the Jewish genocide that swamped Poland. Schindler, a drinker and womaniser, was perhaps light years away from sainthood. Nonetheless, he was rendering service to these hapless Jews, bringing smiles to their faces—and in time, it all paid off.

By 1944, Schindler had transformed, for the most part, into a purpose-driven man. Presumably, he had begun to savour the inner joy of servitude, of bringing happiness to other people's lives. Meanwhile, with the Soviet takeover of Krakow seeming imminent, Berlin ordered operations in Krakow to be closed and the prisoners—including Schindler's

Jews—to be transferred to the infamously brutal Auschwitz camp. However, Schindler, now a purposeful individual, felt compelled to continue assisting the persecuted Jewish community. He opened another factory and a concentration camp—a façade that he named Brinnlitz—near his hometown, where he planned to continue serving the Jews.

With the assistance of his staff, Schindler then bent over backwards to compile a comprehensive list of all those who had worked in his factory, intending to take them to Brinnlitz rather than Auschwitz. But to have a say in who populated his new camp and worked in his new factory—to ensure that the prisoners on his list were the ones to go there—he bribed the SS officer-in-charge with a fortune.

But why was he so particular over his choice of prisoners? What was so special about his list of Jews? Was productivity the motive? Definitely not. His new factory required skills drastically different from those relevant in Krakow. A fresh set of prisoners would in no way affect its output.

To Be Purpose-Driven Is to Be Driven by Love

Presuming that Schindler's sole concern was saving Jewish lives, and productivity was not a consideration, the question remains: why did he squander a fortune to buy out his chosen list of prisoners? Perhaps a better use of that money would have been to purchase more comforts for the Brinnlitz camp—for whosoever occupied it. Although this argument sounds perfectly rational, it wouldn't have resonated with Schindler, for a purposeful life is less about the head and more about the heart. To be purpose-driven is to be driven by love; to serve selflessly means to love. Schindler had built a heart-to-heart connection and a sense of belonging with his Jewish workforce. Consequently, he felt obliged to save their lives at any cost—literally. Later on, when one of the trains supposed to carry his prisoners to Brinnlitz ended up at Auschwitz, Schindler bribed officials with diamonds to reroute it back to his own camp.

While Schindler was finding meaning in Krakow and later at Brinnlitz, another man discovered it at Auschwitz. Viktor Frankl, however, wasn't another kind-hearted Nazi. He was a Jewish prisoner at Auschwitz who survived the Holocaust and shared his experiences in his epic memoir, *Man's Search for Meaning*. How he found meaning amidst the anguish, he relates in his book: "... my mind clung to my wife's image, imagining it with an uncanny acuteness... I grasped the meaning of the greatest secret that human poetry and human thought and belief have to impart—the salvation of man is through love and in love. I understood how a man who has nothing left in this world still may know bliss, be it only for a brief moment, in the contemplation of his beloved." Like Schindler, Frankl too found meaning in love, in a sense of belonging. He lived through the unliveable with the purpose of seeing—and serving—his wife once again.

For most people, discussions of love, belonging, and connection seem incongruous in the world of professionalism. The tacit notion is that losers resort to such tender topics to soothe their wounds. On the other hand, the concept of being purpose-driven or the idea of finding meaning in the workplace is starting to see red carpets in corporate culture. But on close scrutiny, both love and purpose allude to the same basic human condition, though couched differently. Whether we like to believe it or not, all of us—at home or at the office, in our personal or professional lives—are searching for heart-to-heart connections.

"A decade ago, the idea that we are 'wired for connection' might have been perceived as touchy-feely or New Age. Today, we know that the need for connection is more than a feeling or a hunch. It's hard science. Neuroscience, to be exact," writes Brené Brown in *The Gifts of Imperfection*. Bestselling author Mark Manson compares the mind to a car, a Consciousness Car, with two people travelling in it: the Feeling Brain and the Thinking Brain. Put more plainly, we have a rational side to our thinking, and also an emotional side. Manson says that the emotional side, which seeks love, belonging and connection, is the one that drives our Consciousness Car because, "ultimately, we are moved to action only by emotion." And the most powerful and all-encompassing of all emotions being love, it is the one that steers our lives—not just our personal but also our professional.

The Purpose That Drives You Could Be a Humble One

In addition to the insight of the correlation between purpose and love, the stories of Schindler and Frankl show how uncorrelated purpose and grandiosity can be. Schindler saved the lives of just 1,200 Jews, a humble 0.02 per cent of the six million victims of the Holocaust, and Frankl even fewer—just himself. Nevertheless, both serve as heroes for seekers of a meaningful life. To be purpose-driven doesn't necessitate that one puts a dent in the universe. All that counts is one's attitude.

Take another story. That of Alicia, a nobody who lived in a tiny rented frame house in Princeton Junction in the 1970s with her 12-year-old son Johnny and ex-husband John. Both John and Johnny suffered from paranoid schizophrenia, a mental disorder with debilitating symptoms that blur the line between the real and the surreal. John often haunted the Princeton University campus, earning for himself the nickname "Phantom". A silent man walking the halls of the mathematics department night and day, with sunken eyes and a sad, immobile face, the Phantom took to scribbling gibberish on the blackboards that lined the corridors: "Mao Tse-Tung's Bar Mitzvah was 13 years, 13 months and 13 days after Brezhnev's circumcision," or "I agree with Harvard: There is a brain flat." Because he had acquired the distinction of a mathematical genius before schizophrenia had taken the best of him, students who were bookworms and lacked social grace were half-jokingly warned by friends that they too risked winding up like the Phantom. Except for occasional slighting remarks, people for the most part respected him—but from a safe distance.

For Alicia, who juggled her professional life with her domestic chores, accommodating her divorced husband meant going beyond the call of duty. It was irrational to put up with someone who was not only insane, but also derived more pleasure from creative work than from emotional closeness to other people when he was sane. Notwithstanding, Alicia supported him in every possible way. She didn't try to control his behaviour or rather, misbehaviour; she just gave him his space. She was truly purpose-driven. She was driven by love.

By the late 1980s and early 1990s, Alicia's care had a miraculous impact on John's mental health, effectuating a recovery that's unusual for patients with schizophrenia. At around the same time, a paper that John had published in 1950 started to get frequently cited in academic journals on economics. And in 1994, John—whose full name is John Forbes Nash—won the Nobel Prize in Economics for that very paper he had published when he was merely 20.

Going by his biography, authored by Sylvia Nasar, it seemed unlikely that John would be a recipient of the award, had he not made a comeback to a normal life by then. Prize committees are typically less than enthusiastic to invite potential embarrassment on stage during the award ceremony by calling up a deranged mathematician.

Following John's rise to glory, Alicia, the real hero in his life story, has offered hope to countless caregivers of those mentally challenged and has inspired homemakers across the globe. Her example demonstrates that love has the power to heal, that even seemingly lacklustre occupations can transform lives, and that leading a purposeful life is indeed worthwhile.

In the same vein, the biography of Victor Frankl helps millions find meaning in their lives. By the time he died in 1997, *Man's Search for Meaning* had sold over 16 million copies and had been translated into 24 languages. Now, more than

70 years after its publication, it still occupies a prominent display in bookstores around the world. It also belongs to a list of "the ten most influential books in the United States."

As for Oskar Schindler's life story, author Thomas Keneally did narrate it through his writings, allowing millions to read it. The person who had inspired him to write, shopkeeper Leopold Page, was among the Jews saved by Schindler. Page had been pushing hard to sell his idea to any author he encountered. Keneally was the fortunate one who relented. The book that Keneally wrote, *Schindler's Ark*, was later dramatised into a biopic by the famed Hollywood director Steven Spielberg in 1993. His film, *Schindler's List*, continues to inspire millions around the globe to lead a purpose-driven life, a life of love.

11

FINDING RECIPROCATION FOR BEING PURPOSE-DRIVEN

Do You Feel That You Are Appreciated and Your Love Is Requited?

On August 12, 1960, the US embassy in Moscow received an unusual letter from a member of the upper echelons of Soviet Military Intelligence. "It is a good friend who is turning to you, a friend who has already become your soldier-warrior for the cause of truth, for the ideals of a truly free world, and democracy for mankind." This defector claimed he was disgusted with the communist regime, which he thought was a catastrophic circus of scoundrels with Soviet Premier Nikita Khrushchev as their ringmaster—and the citizens paying dearly for the show, whether they liked it or not. This military colonel from the Soviet Republic claimed he had top, relevant, and urgent military secrets to share. He was offering to spy for the West. The CIA, Central Intelligence Agency of the United States, possibly swathed in misgivings, did not respond to this first overture by Colonel Oleg Penkovsky. MI6, the UK intelligence agency, however, eagerly accepted his offer when it came their way. Being allies, the UK and the US eventually decided to run him jointly.

Penkovsky, who found meaning in his life of espionage, went on to play a critical role when the simmering Cold War came to a boil. The secrets that he shared eventually saved the world from the greatest nuclear crisis of all time, when life on earth came perilously close to annihilation.

The first secret meeting with Penkovsky was held at the Mount Royal Hotel in London, where Harry Shergold of the UK and Joe Bulik of the US sounded him out. "To adopt a new people, to fight for a new ideal, for democracy... your cause is my cause," Penkovsky expressed his purpose. He warned them that Soviet Premier Nikita Khrushchev was the "Atomic Hitler" who had given himself the task of instigating a nuclear war. Khrushchev had sworn to "bury Western imperialism under a rain of missiles." What impressed Shergold and Bulik the most were the documents of the Soviet nuclear programme that Penkovsky shared with them. Penkovsky returned to Russia after promising them access to more classified information.

Through his close contacts in the Soviet army, Penkovsky obtained a pass to the library that tightly held military secrets—thoughts of the Soviet High Command, thousands of pages of armament details, and diagrams of missile designs. He routinely visited the library, photographed the pages and diagrams, and through meticulously planned "chance meetings" with people connected to the British embassy, slipped this unparalleled wealth of information to the West. It was through Penkovsky that the US discovered Soviet deployment of nuclear weapons in East Germany. And it was Penkovsky who first revealed that Cuba was being armed by the Soviets—long before anyone in the West even dreamt of it.

The Need for Feeling Appreciated

On July 18, 1961, Penkovsky arrived in London for another secret meeting with his handlers, Shergold and Bulik. Around the same time, Soviet cosmonaut Yuri Gagarin had become the first human to journey into outer space. He was also in London, having been invited by the Queen.

"If you think I have done good work for you, I demand to meet your President," said Penkovsky to Bulik. "... and your Queen," he added, turning to Shergold. When Shergold expressed that it might not be possible, Penkovsky banged the table in a frenzy and raged, "Gagarin dines with the Queen! Has he done more work for you than me? Is he a soldier in your army?"

Penkovsky had been investing his love in the UK and the US, risking his very life. He had come to identify himself as a soldier of the Western forces, purpose-driven to protect them from Soviet nuclear strikes. But he now felt let down; perhaps his sacrifice was not appreciated enough.

"You are our soldier," Shergold reassured Penkovsky. Then, as if substantiating what he had just said, Shergold took Penkovsky aside and had him wear the uniform of a British General. Bulik quickly snapped two photos of Penkovsky donned in full regalia, and these photos can still be found in the CIA archives. In the first snapshot, Penkovsky looks placated. In the second, he holds a boyish smile, akin to a child who has just been appreciated.

That feeling of being valued is the lifeblood of someone who is purpose-driven. If you are rendering selfless service of some sort, and it is being acknowledged by the party at the receiving end or by the world, be grateful. For without that reciprocation, you will not be able to continue with your purposeful attitude for long. But you cannot demand that appreciation either—for that would diminish its flavour. However, when it comes of its own accord, never shy away; just embrace it. Understand that the need of your heart is not just to love but also to be loved. If you, on the other hand, are on the receiving end of selfless love, know that the minimum you can do to reciprocate is to appreciate whoever is offering it. Though those appreciative words cost you nothing, they will be invaluable for the hearts that hear them.

The Need to Feel That Your Love Is Requited

Returning to Penkovsky, his story took a left turn when Cuba became the flashpoint of the Cold War in November of 1961. With the hostility between the East and the West reaching an unprecedented high, the KGB, the Soviet secret police, started keeping close tabs on those connected with US and British embassies, and Penkovsky, who used these Westerners to smuggle out secret information, soon came under the KGB's scrutiny.

Penkovsky was quick to detect that he was being tailed. He sent a message to his handlers requesting that his secret meeting with the Westerners be postponed for three to four months until the dust settled. Shergold was not happy with the idea. He confided in Bulik that with the Cold War intensifying, they needed Penkovsky's espionage now more than ever before. If the embassy personnel did get into trouble, they could safely be called back to the UK, as they had "diplomatic immunity". To this, Bulik protested: "What about Penkovsky? We've got to protect him too, and keep him back for the really big things. He is our soldier..."

But Shergold interrupted—"He is only our agent."

Fortunately or unfortunately, for Penkovsky, this conversation occurred behind his back. As requested by his handlers, he continued with his operations, naively believing that they considered him as one among them—a soldier of the righteous West.

Eventually, as the KGB closed in, a flustered Penkovsky reached out to the UK requesting help: he and his family sought to escape from the USSR.

No help from the UK, however, came by.

But the US did respond. A forged passport that called Penkovsky by a different name arrived from the US. He could use it to travel across the country and make arrangements for him and his family to escape from the USSR. Penkovsky was overwhelmed by the timely help.

While appreciation is one way of reciprocating love, help rendered in times of need is another. That act, however big or small, strengthens love and motivates the receiver to be more purposeful and selfless.

"I am not disappointed with my life or work," wrote Penkovsky to Bulik the day he received his new passport. "If I succeed in contributing my little brick to our great cause, there can be no greater satisfaction. It's not advisable to cease photography (of secret documents) now. It's necessary to continue this work, until they take away my pass (to the library holding military secrets)."

Meanwhile, on the other side of the planet, the US spy planes detected Soviet nuclear missiles piling up in Cuba. The "Cuban Missile Crisis" was on. The pressing questions that gave the CIA cold feet were many. How serious a threat were these missiles? How far could they reach? And how long would it take for the Soviet army to assemble them? This is when the photos sent by Penkovsky filled in the puzzle. They revealed that the missiles from Cuba could reach every corner of the USA and would take four to eight weeks to assemble. When President Kennedy received this information, he called off his orders for the invasion of Cuba. And in doing so, he pulled back the world from the edge of a suicidal leap.

Had he proceeded with Operation Mongoose, the rehearsed plan for the invasion of Cuba, the "Atomic Hitler" Khrushchev would have seized the opportunity to launch a nuclear attack on the US. The US, in turn, would retaliate by launching nuclear attacks on the USSR from its missile bases in Italy, Britain, and Turkey. The result would be another World War—a global nuclear war!

While Kennedy was busy averting the potential catastrophe, the man who played a key role in helping the US president make the timely decision found himself in crisis, neck-deep. The KGB arrested Penkovsky for treason, and it was a foregone conclusion that he would soon be executed.

One day, while Penkovsky was held in a prison in Moscow, Bulik approached the CIA chief in Washington DC with the report of Penkovsky's arrest. The chief was concerned—would Penkovsky disclose any US military secrets? Bulik reassured him—"He is too loyal." "We've got to get him back by negotiating a deal," he added.

"It's not going to happen," replied the chief.

"We overuse him, then we drop him? He is our soldier!" retorted Bulik.

"He has done a great job. But he was on the wrong side," said the CIA chief.

Penkovsky was executed on May 16, 1963, in his Moscow confinement.

He was, of course, appreciated by the people he loved and sacrificed for. But he had also experienced the heartbreak of a cold response from the UK when he had pleaded for help. And worst of all, he would have been shattered by the betrayal of the people he selflessly served, had he known that after all he had done for them, he was still considered only an "agent" and not their "soldier".

The Conundrum of a Purpose-Driven Life

As purpose-driven as you may be, and no matter the extent of your sincerity, you cannot always expect the world, or the people you have served and loved, to wait on you with a bowl of cherries. In the story of Penkovsky, that lack of reciprocation was deliberate. But even when no one intends to, fate can devise other ways to disappoint you.

Consider the small group of Nazi soldiers who were part of the failed plot to assassinate Hitler on July 20, 1944. They bore the stigma of being viewed as traitors. The very country they intended to save from a mindless dictator failed to appreciate their cause. That was because Germany, still entranced by Hitler's harangue, failed to hear the Soviet tanks fast approaching Berlin. The few Germans who did appreciate these rebels were too small a number, most of them civilians, who could only watch in horror—needless to say, they could offer no help—as their heroes were executed for the attempted assassination of the Führer.

Ignaz Semmelweis, the Hungarian doctor of the nineteenth century who pioneered antiseptic procedures, was never appreciated by the medical fraternity of his time. Although he practically demonstrated how hand washing by doctors reduced the spread of fatal infections, thereby saving the lives of thousands, he failed to back his findings with scientific explanations; the medical science back then had no knowledge of the underworld of disease-causing microbes that deceived the naked eye. Consequently, Semmelweis was rejected and ridiculed, and his recommendations were met with scepticism and scorn. Not that his peers disparaged him deliberately; they simply failed to catch up with someone who was way ahead of his time. Crying alone in the wilderness, Semmelweis died a disappointed man at the age of 47 in a mental asylum, to which he was committed because the medical community thought he was insane.

Christine Collins was a woman whose nine-year-old son went missing on March 10, 1928, from their home in Los Angeles. From that point on, her sole purpose in life was to find him. In 1964, she died a disappointed mother, who never found the reciprocation of her love. The fate of her son remains a mystery to this day.

Whether that selflessness is in relation to humanity, nationality, community or family, the failure to be appreciated, to be let down, or even to be betrayed—whether intentionally or unintentionally—is all too commonplace.

In the corporate world, particularly, treachery is widespread.

Some years ago, a board member of a multimillion-dollar corporation started attending my weekly classes on the Bhagavad Gita held at ISKCON Chowpatty, Mumbai. Like most of his ilk, he was initially reticent. However, he soon let down his guard, and our conversations grew more informal. As it turned out, this man was a high-ranking executive with several thousand white-collar employees at his beck and call. He had been loyally serving his company for over two decades, overseeing its growth from infancy to the giant it had become. A multinational was now poised to acquire the corporation, and the prospect seemed dazzlingly bright. I could tell without missing a beat that this man's singular purpose in life was to make his company great.

A few days after he had filled me in about the acquisition, he called me late at night. In a tremulous voice that revealed despair, he expressed a desire to meet me as soon as possible. Within half an hour, I found myself sitting on a park bench, listening to him as he unwound a tale of betrayal by his colleagues. They had plotted against him in the wake of the merger, cornering him into resigning. He was heartbroken, and so was I.

In the months that followed, I was his friendly ear, into which he poured out his sullen heart, and I was his spiritual eyes through which he strained to see the silver lining in the dark clouds that loomed over him.

For me, the whole episode confirmed what I already knew. A purpose-driven attitude could be as much a curse as it could be a blessing. The more-than-perfect stories of Oskar Schindler or Alicia Nash—wherein purposeful attitudes and love were reciprocated to a T—are undoubtedly inspiring, but they are not the norm. A meaningful life—more often than not—does not pan out the way we envision it. Love often remains unrequited, many times betrayed, culminating in endless suffering. Perhaps we all know this truth subconsciously, and so we prefer to remain mere cheerleaders of the bravehearts who enter the arena of selfless sacrifice for the sake of their community, their company, their nation, or humanity; and we are loath to venture out ourselves. But hiding behind that cover of selfishness—is that a decent or intelligent alternative? As we have discussed at length before, it is certainly not.

So here we are, stuck. On one side is the devil of selfishness. And on the other is the deep sea of selflessness—beautiful, but with ubiquitous undercurrents of uncertainty. Which side do we turn to? What is the way out of this conundrum?

12

INVESTING YOURSELF IN MORE THAN ONE PURPOSE

Is That a Better Option?

On March 21, 1975, two Israeli secret agents, Avner and Steve, walked into a bank in Geneva to settle an account into which millions of dollars had flowed in the past two and a half years. That money had been funding a mission they were a part of, but the operation had just been called off. After closing that account, the two decided to retain their personal accounts containing $100,000 each. Their monthly salaries from the Mossad, the national intelligence agency of Israel, had trickled into their respective accounts during the years of the operation, adding up to that modest amount.

But a few months later, when the two returned, all that was left in Avner's account was three dollars, while Steve's remained untouched with $100,000. The Mossad had pulled back Avner's cumulative salary, leaving him bankrupt. Was he caught spying against his country? Had he attempted to play foul with the Mossad? No to both. His only "crime" was that in the intervening months, he had decided to quit the secret service, wanting to start afresh with a new profession in a new country—the United States.

Standing on the dark green marble floor inside that bank in Geneva, Avner could hardly breathe. His limbs and lips trembled. The thought of maintaining a family of three with three dollars unnerved him. He felt betrayed by his own people.

From his side, he had been purpose-driven for his country throughout. When he was barely 23, he had walked away from his pregnant wife into a dangerous mission with no certainty of when he would return, or whether he would return at all. He had embarked on a secretive mission that he would never be publicly acknowledged for being a part of, which in and of itself eliminated any odds of winning glory, honour, or medals for himself. It was never about the money either. That went without saying. Only a fool would sign up for a life-threatening gig for the less-than-modest salary the Mossad offered. In fact, the thought of remuneration hadn't even crossed his mind until his officer had mentioned it during the briefing at the beginning of the mission: "Whenever you are in Switzerland, you can look at your account and see it grow."

Even now, when the operation was over, he wasn't longing for the money per se. His sacrifice was for his country, and it remained that way. Nonetheless, the stark ground reality was that he needed something to support his family—his wife and his daughter. Couldn't the Mossad understand that? Had all the good he had done to date been erased from their database just because he had resigned? The withdrawal of his salary betrayed their ingratitude.

When Avner landed in New York City, where his wife and daughter now lived, he didn't even have the money to travel home. His wife Soshana came to the airport to pick him up. On the way home, with Soshana behind the wheel, Avner filled her in with all that had happened. And in the same breath, hoping to make her feel better, added that his new plan was to rejoin the Mossad. Soshana's response came as a surprise. She screeched the car to a halt and screamed "no". Then, with a bolt of lightning flashing from her eyes, she added, "I'd rather scrub floors for a living. But I won't allow them to force it upon you!" Avner could tell she unquestionably meant every word she said.

Try to Be Purpose-Driven Both in Personal Life and Professional Life

Avner's officers had bitterly betrayed him, no doubt, but at home sweet Soshana was there by his side to offset that bitterness. She loved him no matter what. Being purposeful at the workplace had misfired, but his home promised to requite his love spot on.

Remember the distraught corporate executive who was cheated by the company he gave his life for? His story roughly took the same turn as Avner's. As he sat beside me on a park bench a few days after he was cornered to resign, I asked him, my heart palpitating, "I hope you aren't haunted by thoughts of suicide!" He looked up at me, his elbows resting on his knees, and his back still stooped over, "How can I think of suicide, when I know my little daughter still needs me?" Then he added wistfully, "I now wish I had given more time to my family all these years. But from now on, I have resolved to."

Both these stories reiterate the well-worn wisdom of work-life balance but also offer a fresh perspective for one in search of meaning. It's wise to invest your love and find a purpose, both at home and at the workplace. If one investment fails, the other will likely cover you up.

In both of these stories, it was the home that was the saving grace. But for that lady whom we briefly met in the previous chapter—Christine Collins—whose nine-year-old son went missing, it was just the opposite. Life at home without her only son was traumatising.

As Collins struggled to find meaning at home, a well-wisher suggested that she step out and take up the mission of cleaning up the Los Angeles Police Department. The corrupt department wasn't just lax in their search for the missing boy but had stooped so low that in their attempts to skirt their responsibility, had set up a look-alike to be Collins' son. When she protested, saying that the boy wasn't her son, they had audaciously committed her to a mental asylum.

"Mrs. Collins, a lot of mothers' sons have been sacrificed to expediency around here," the well-wisher told her. "Your son, unfortunately, would not be the first. But if you do it right, he may very well be the last." Those words gave Collins a new purpose in life. She went to the courts, took the police department to task, and made Los Angeles a safer place for both mothers and children alike. She earned the love and respect of an entire city. She had lost her purpose within the walls of her home but had found another when she had marched out of the door.

What If You Don't Find Reciprocation from Anywhere?

And yet, there are umpteen stories of those who found the reciprocation of their love neither inside the home nor outside of it. Take Alan Turing, the British mathematical genius who played a cardinal role in World War II. Turing was the primary force behind breaking the secret codes aired out every day from Berlin to the Nazi army on the warfront. Turing's team relayed the decoded messages to the British Intelligence, helping them understand the enemy's strategy in advance and gain the upper hand. According to historians today, Turing is credited with shortening the war in Europe by two years, thus saving 14 million lives. But back then, because of the Official Secrets Act of the British government, Turing's contributions were destined to remain a secret for the next 50 years. He was to remain unappreciated and unloved for his mammoth purpose-driven war efforts, perhaps for as long as he lived. Unfortunately, unlike Avner, he didn't have a family to turn to because he was gay. And worse, playing by the laws of the land extant at that time, his government publicly humiliated him for his unorthodox sexual orientation. Presumably, unable to take it all, Turing committed suicide in 1954, at age 41.

Truth be told, despite finding love alternatives, even Collins and Avner never entirely got over their heartbreaks either. Collins continued to pine for her lost son for the rest of her life. And Avner, unable to swallow the injustice that his office had inflicted, resorted to *Vengeance*.

Avner's experiences during the clandestine operation and his feelings of betrayal afterwards were articulated by the author George Jonas in the international bestseller *Vengeance*, published in 1984. The book's title ostensibly refers to the mission headed by Avner that avenged the assassination of Israeli athletes by Palestinian terrorists during the 1972 Munich Olympics. But in addition to chronicling the thrilling details of the counterterrorist operation itself, the book airs Israel's dirty laundry in public by surfacing the deep biases rampant in the country's bureaucracy. In fact, it was this bigotry, more than any other factor, that had discomforted Avner to the point of his resigning from the Mossad. By bringing his story of betrayal to the public, Avner had taken vengeance against his officers.

In doing so, had he wronged? Arguably, he had, because he had disclosed a lot of his country's classified information. But it was also a fact that he was being forced to bite the bullet. A lot of purpose-driven people, in spite of themselves, succumb to wrongdoing when they don't feel reciprocated with. It's not too uncommon a phenomenon.

When the heart remains dreary despite the sacrifices we have made, we turn around to be self-centred once again. The soul is pleasure-seeking—*ananda mayo bhyasat*—if we can't find it internally, we once again scour for it in the externals. And now, with greater vehemence, in a hurry to make up for the external opportunities that we lost while futilely giving a shot at being internal. That sour feeling that we forfeited so much to no avail can often trigger revenge fantasies—directed against the very people we once sacrificed for.

Finding a promising purpose we can dedicate our lives to is one of the greatest enigmas of human existence.

13

IS YOUR PURPOSE-DRIVEN LIFE ON A SLIPPERY SLOPE?

The Dangers of Not Finding a Worthy Purpose

On April 30, 1975, the Vietcong, the army that had waged a guerrilla war against the American forces, triumphantly marched into Saigon, the South Vietnamese capital. The event marked the end of the Vietnam War. James Fenton, a journalist from England who witnessed it all, later recalled it as "an occasion of overt celebration." In common with many people across the planet, he admired the Vietcong as a nationalist movement and believed the Americans had not the slightest justification for their interference in Indochina.

Slipping Down from Being Purpose-Driven to Being Want-Driven

After the takeover, Fenton stayed around long enough in Saigon to see the shape that the post-war era took. To his dismay, the new regime was totalitarian. They took over the schools and universities, they shut down the free press, and they pursued programmes of enforced relocation. Many South Vietnamese were sent elsewhere, supposedly for re-education—and most of them never returned. The few who made it back home were brought in coffins. "The victory of the Vietnamese was a victory for Stalinism," Fenton wrote poignantly in an article published years later.

Stalinism refers to Joseph Stalin's style of governance during his rule over the Soviet Union. His political career seems to have begun with pure motives of liberating the commoners from the oppressive Tsar regime. His sacrifices were indeed appreciated by the masses, who loved him to the point of adulation. That's how he meteorically rose to power, to become the premier of the Union. Nonetheless, in the later part of his life, his governance was driven more by a want for power than by a sense of purpose. In the end, he left behind a legacy of selfish tyranny sugar-coated with the grand idea of selfless communism.

In the same vein, the Soviet Red Army of World War II was initially purpose-driven to end the Nazi persecution of Jews in Eastern Europe. They liberated many concentration camps, including the one at Auschwitz, and were looked upon as messiahs by the prisoners they released. Its Commander Vasily Petrenkov expressed shock over the Nazis' indescribable hatred even towards women, children, and old men. But when the same army marched into Berlin, they themselves became the perpetrators. *A Woman in Berlin*, a memoir by the journalist Marta Hillers, describes the widespread rapes of German women and the inhuman treatment of old German men by the in-marching Soviet troops.

How is it that people slip from the slopes of a purposeful life despite their love being requited? On the battlefield of Kurukshetra, when Sri Krishna advocated a purpose-driven life, Arjuna asked the same pressing question, though framed differently.

> Arjuna asked: O Krishna, by what is one impelled to act wrongly, even unwillingly, as if engaged by force? (Bhagavad Gita 3.36)

> Lord Sri Krishna replied: It is the intense passion for wants which is the enemy within pushing one towards wrongdoings. These fierce wants, when unfulfilled, transform into wrath. (Bhagavad Gita 3.37)

Slipping Further from Being Want-Driven to Being Wrath-Driven

The tendency to be want-driven is deeply rooted; the thirst for external pleasures is primitive. They can re-erupt like dormant volcanoes, even when we are sincerely trying to be purpose-driven. And when that lava of lust does resurface, if not assuaged, it burns as anger. It bewilders us.

> The senses, the mind and the intelligence are the sitting places of this lust. Through them, lust covers the real knowledge of the living entity and bewilders him. (Bhagavad Gita 3.40)

It was under the sway of that anger and bewilderment, induced by his lust for power, that India's freedom fighter, Mohammad Ali Jinnah, pronounced, "We shall have India divided, or we shall have India destroyed." That clarion call instigated Muslim mobs to burst from their slums in Calcutta, waving clubs, iron bars, and shovels on the dawn of August 16, 1946, which Jinnah's Muslim League called the Direct Action Day. The Muslims set Hindu neighbourhoods aflame and bludgeoned any Hindu they could lay their hands upon. Later, the Hindu mobs stormed out of their neighbourhoods too, looking for defenceless Muslims to slaughter. Authors Larry Collins and Dominique Lapierre vividly describe that sordid day in their international bestseller, *Freedom at Midnight*:

> Like water-soaked logs, scores of bloated corpses bobbed down the Hooghly river towards the sea. Others, savagely mutilated, littered the city's streets… By the time the slaughter was over, Calcutta belonged to the vultures. In filthy grey packs, they scudded across the sky, tumbling down to gorge themselves on the bodies of the city's 6,000 dead.

In 1904, when Jinnah joined the Indian National Congress, a nationalist movement that struggled for India's independence, he seemed purpose-driven. Perhaps he truly was. Back then, he was a proponent of not just a free India, but also of a united India in which Hindus and Muslims lived peacefully together. In fact, in 1933, when a person named Rahamat Ali first approached him with the idea of a separate state called Pakistan, Jinnah, remaining true to his ideals, dismissed the concept as an "impossible dream". Perhaps even he didn't know back then, to what extent the lust for power lay dormant within him.

That want-driven attitude in Jinnah, that he had repressed for so long, broke free as India came closer to her freedom.

Judging by his sudden change of stance in 1937, it appeared as though he was pushed by it—almost unwillingly. He became an ardent advocate of a divided India almost overnight, as soon as it became clear that he stood no chance of becoming a political honcho in a united India. His lust for power hungered for something to feed on—if not the post of the prime minister of an entire nation, then at least the head of one of its factions. And when the leaders of the Congress and of the British Empire remained adamant on keeping India united after her freedom, that lust in Jinnah transformed into the wrath that killed 6,000 people on the streets of Calcutta on August 16, 1946. But that was just a prelude to what came exactly a year later. On August 15, 1947, when the freedom of India coincided with its partition, an estimated 2,00,000 to 20,00,000 people were killed in the Hindu-Muslim riots that ensued.

The story of Jinnah echoes that of Harvey Dent, a fictional character in the Hollywood blockbuster of 2008, *The Dark Knight*. While Jinnah was driven to wrongdoing by the lust for power, Dent was driven by the lust for vengeance. While Jinnah was a leader in India, Dent was the district attorney of the fictitious city of Gotham. Both began as purpose-driven individuals but both ended up as deranged killers. Dent directly murdered a handful, while Jinnah indirectly caused the deaths of a few million. "I took Gotham's white knight and brought him down to our level," says Joker, the villain who catalysed Dent's fall from grace. "It wasn't hard. You see, madness, as you know, is like gravity. All it takes is a little push."

The vulnerability of the human psyche couldn't be articulated better. The scriptwriter truly did a remarkable job.

The want-driven side in all of us, the selfish lust within, is like gravity that's relentlessly trying to pull our consciousness down to materialism. Only if the purpose-driven side of us powerfully imbues us with selfless love, can our consciousness escape past that gravitational field and ascend into the outer space of spiritual freedom. To be purpose-driven is important, but to find a purpose that's strong enough to resist temptations is more crucial. Else, we could end up becoming a far worse villain than the good-enough hero we set out to become.

Capturing the essence of this chapter and the previous ones, in which we delved deeper into the concept of "purpose", this is my concluding remark:

To be purpose-driven is to be driven by love. Our need is not just to love, but also to be loved. That's the deepest calling of the soul. So, the cause to which we are giving our hearts should be worthy of it. We need to be sure that we will be appreciated; that our love will be reciprocated, not betrayed. And the inner satisfaction and fulfilment we experience through that love will be strong enough to offset all negativity within and powerful enough to resist external temptations that will invariably attempt to lure us back to our old want-driven ways.

The Bhagavad Gita provides us with a cause so worthy that it will honour our dedication. A purpose that's deeper than the oceans, higher than the skies, and wider than the horizon. And what that is, we shall discuss in the next chapter.

14

THE PURPOSE THAT DRIVES A KARMA YOGI

Transcendental Service

In the first week of May 1945, as World War II raged in full fury, the 77th division of the US army was in the Pacific, immersed in an operation larger than that of D-Day. Their mission was codenamed Iceberg, and its objective—to wrest the island of Okinawa from the Japanese stronghold.

Okinawa served as a Japanese military headquarters with ample food, ammunition, and weapons. The soldiers stationed there far outnumbered the 77th division; their defence tactics were ruthless, and their spirits undying. Furthermore, the Americans were seriously challenged by the island's unusual terrain. The majority of the isle stood on a plateau, and to even reach it, their army had to climb an escarpment—a wall of rock—300 feet high. Most of the time, the Japanese shot down an American the moment he climbed atop that ridge. Sometimes, the Japanese strategically waited until a large concentration of US soldiers had scaled the escarpment and occupied a segment of that rocky plateau. Then they opened fire with everything they had, killing and wounding dozens of American soldiers and chasing the rest back down the ridge. Nine times in seven days, American forces were driven off the escarpment; eight company commanders were killed in less than 36 hours; platoons of 30 men had returned with only five or six. With all odds stacked against them, even the titans of the 77th Division had their morale ripped apart in Operation Iceberg.

It was under such dire circumstances that an unassuming, wiry medic rose to the occasion and inspired his division. His name was Desmond Doss.

On May 5, 1945, 155 men of the 77th Division—Desmond Doss among them—managed to climb up the escarpment. It was their third attempt at gaining a foothold on the isle. But again, as in their previous attempts, the Japanese came in hordes and opened a brutal barrage of artillery, grenade, mortar, and rifle fire. Fifty-five Americans retreated and climbed down the ridge hastily, back to safety. One hundred were left behind on the top, some of whom were killed; others were wounded and struggled to find cover in foxholes as they continued to fight back. Desmond Doss wasn't wounded, but he wasn't willing to climb down either. He wasn't prepared to leave a single injured soldier behind, knowing well that after nightfall the Japanese would scout the place for the wounded with the intent of torturing them.

What Doss did in the next 12 hours was nothing short of a miracle. Amid the hail of fire and the swarm of bullets, Doss dragged the wounded soldiers one by one to the edge of the escarpment and lowered them down with a rope, back to safety. Some of those men he had to haul as far as 125 yards before roping them down. All the while, he could hear concerned calls from below the ridge—"Doss, get down!"—but he paid no heed to them. In all, he ended up saving 75 lives, for which he was later awarded the Congressional Medal of Honor, the highest military honour of the United States.

Desmond Doss was purpose-driven. That's for sure. But what was the purpose he stood for? Apparently, he was purpose-driven to serve his country. That answer seems obvious at first. But if we give the background of this story the attention it is due, we will realise there is more to it than meets the eye.

Being Driven by a Purpose That's All-Encompassing

It was in April of 1942, approximately three years before Operation Iceberg, that Doss had joined the infantry. He was keen on serving his country in the war effort despite being a *conscientious objector*—someone who refused to bear arms because of his religious beliefs. Heading for a war without weapons may have sounded meaningless to others, but Doss had a clear plan of action in mind—while his comrades would be busy taking lives on the battlegrounds, he would be right by their side saving lives as a military medic. Though his thinking fell in line with the American constitution, it didn't sit well with his comrades. They regarded his attitude as holier-than-thou and alienated him. He was the butt of jokes and ridicule.

After the day-drills, as he sat in the evening by his bedstead, reading the Holy Bible, shoes would be hurled at him.

Even his commanding officers were persistent about him undergoing rifle training so that he could carry at least a .45 calibre on the warfront like the other medics. And when he resisted, he was singled out as a pest and the weakest link of the division. They were keen on ousting him, not just from the regiment, but also from the American army.

Meanwhile, in mid-1943, the company was transferred to Camp Hyder in Arizona for desert training. Despite the temperature soaring up to 54 degrees, the infantry would be sent on drills with just one canteen of water. With conditions so harsh, desertion became commonplace. Some soldiers ran off into the desert, never to be seen again. But Doss was there to stay. And it was at Camp Hyder that he first made his mark. He always put his men first: sharing his ration of water, treating the raw and blistered feet of his comrades, and caring for those who had dehydration or sunstroke. When he wrote to the captain requesting more water supply for the men to beat the heat, his wish was granted, but he in turn had to bear the temper of his immediate superior. By directly contacting the captain, he had breached the line of command and unwittingly slighted his company commander.

All in all, despite his outstanding service attitude, Desmond still found himself challenged by the commanding officers of the American army. Contrary to reasoning, they started to grow less tolerant of his refusal to carry arms. He was threatened with court martial, was placed on permanent KP duty where he scrubbed pots and pans until his hands were raw pieces of meat, and was denied passes to visit his newly-wedded wife. On one occasion, when Doss approached his captain with the furlough papers, wanting to go home to see off his younger brother heading for the Navy, the officer tore off the documents instead of signing them. Most of Doss's colleagues neither appreciated him nor reciprocated his kindness. If at all he received anything in return for all the good he did for his country, it was betrayal. And yet, of the 75 countrymen he saved during Operation Iceberg—while putting his own life at stake—many were men who had ridiculed and roasted him during the training. Had Doss not been driven by the sole purpose of serving his country, it was highly unlikely that he could have done what he did.

Like Avner, the Israeli secret agent who turned vengeful against his own side, Doss would be struggling with negative thoughts against his own men. Or else, like Alan Turing, the British mathematical genius who was crestfallen by how he was mistreated by his countrymen, Doss, too, would be heartbroken by how he was maltreated. Either way, he couldn't have held on to a selfless attitude, and that too on the battlefield where his own life was on the line. And even if he tried, he couldn't have resisted the temptation when his few well-wishers from below the ridge advised him to descend down to safety. He would have latched on to every excuse to climb down that escarpment, leaving behind his perpetrators to die at the hands of the Japanese.

Doss was undoubtedly driven by a deeper purpose, a cause so powerful that it warded off all feelings of resentment and hate even towards those who abused him, and replaced those toxic emotions with positivity and love. But what was it?

Doss himself leads us to the answer in *The Conscientious Objector*, a documentary about his life produced in 2004. At the age of 85, Doss can be seen recollecting and revealing what transpired in his mind as he dragged those 75 men back to safety. "Please Lord, help me get one more. Please Lord, help me get one more..." That had been his constant prayer throughout those 12 hours, as he pulled out soldier after soldier from the jaws of death.

Doss was purpose-driven to serve God, to love God. Whether or not he received appreciation and reciprocation from the people he served and saved was secondary. What really mattered to him was the tangible inner fulfilment he experienced for having served God's will. That spiritual joy sprung from his soul, from beneath the superficial layers of the senses and the mind, and strengthened his resolve to remain purpose-driven even in the face of temptations.

> The working senses are superior to dull matter; mind is higher than the senses; intelligence is still higher than the mind; and the soul is even higher than the intelligence. Thus knowing oneself to be transcendental to the material senses, mind and intelligence, O mighty-armed Arjuna, one should steady the mind by deliberate spiritual intelligence and thus—by spiritual strength—conquer the tendency to be want-driven. (Bhagavad Gita 3.42, 3.43)

This "deliberate spiritual intelligence" that Sri Krishna speaks about was elaborated upon by Mother Teresa when she said:

> People are often unreasonable, illogical and self-centred. Forgive them anyway. If you are kind, people may accuse you of

selfish, ulterior motives. Be kind anyway. If you are successful, you will win some false friends and some true enemies. Succeed anyway. If you are honest and frank, people may cheat you. Be honest and frank anyway. What you spend years building, someone could destroy overnight. Build anyway. If you find serenity and happiness, they may be jealous. Be happy anyway. The good you do today, people will often forget tomorrow. Do good anyway. Give the world the best you have, and it may never be enough. Give your best anyway. You see, in the final analysis, it is between you and your God. It was never between you and them anyway.

Long ago, on the battlefield of Kurukshetra, Arjuna too was asked to make his purpose of life, service to God. And fortunately for him, that very God stood in front of him. It was Sri Krishna, roleplaying as his charioteer and now speaking the Bhagavad Gita.

> Lord Sri Krishna said: Be purpose-driven to serve me. With full knowledge of me, without a selfish agenda, without any sense of being the doer, and without lethargy, fight. (Bhagavad Gita 3.30)

When we are purpose-driven to serve God in this way, we are acting in Karma Yoga.

PART IV

Advancing in Karma Yoga

15

HARNESS THE POWER OF SIMPLICITY
Its Five Benefits

The date was August 6, 2019, and the time was close to sundown. After leading *katha* and *kirtan* in a lavish apartment perched on the 55th floor of a high-end residential tower in South Mumbai, I was preparing to leave. My host, the CEO of a top investment bank, graciously offered to drop me back to the ashram. He escorted me down to the basement and showed me to his sleek BMW X3. After I occupied the passenger seat, a boy who had joined me for the event, hopped into the rear. The 10-year-old was proficient in Indian classical drums, so I had taken him along for accompaniment during kirtan. He hailed from a middle-class family that lived close to our ashram.

My host slipped behind the wheels and turned on the ignition. The car's engine revved in a mellifluous hum, and the majestic vehicle cruised ahead at a leisurely pace, past the security gate. No sooner did it hit the road than the high-pitched voice of the boy rang out from the rear seat:

"*Prabhuji, main pehli baar luxury car mein baitha hoon*" (I am sitting in a luxury car for the first time in my life). Struggling to hide my wince, I turned a deaf ear. A few awkward moments of silence passed by. At last, my host, realising my embarrassment, struck up a conversation to put me at ease. The boy, meanwhile, oblivious to any feelings of unease, went about exploring the stand-out features of the vehicle for the rest of the ride.

The incident is indelible for me, for that day I grasped the essence of "childlike simplicity" in full measure. The essence of simplicity is this: to have one's thoughts, words, and actions perfectly aligned. My young friend had played that out unwittingly, and so adorably. When the thought occurred to him that he had never ridden in a luxury car before, he unhesitatingly verbalised it and guilelessly went about marvelling at the car's interiors. He couldn't care less about concealing his thoughts through his words or actions.

A Simple Person Is Unabashed by Reversals

Ever wondered why children are good learners? The reasons are manifold, but one surely stands out. Because a child is simple-hearted, he neither hides his failures nor his imperfections. God forbid, if he did, he wouldn't even learn to walk. He would forever be sitting tight, for fear that if he fell while taking his baby steps, his shortcomings would be exposed.

Simplicity allows you to admit your limitations and work wholeheartedly on overcoming them. That's how you give failures a fair chance to act as springboards to successes. Sample the following case study from my own ashram:

My ashram adjoins the ISKCON temple at Marine Drive in South Mumbai—Sri Sri Radhagopinath Temple. Both the temple and the monastery were established by my guru, Radhanath Swami, in 1986, and both flourished under his guidance. The number of resident monks in the ashram steadily rose to hundreds, and the size of the temple congregation who visited on weekends exponentially grew to thousands. In the year 2000, a documentary was made on the success of the community by filmmaker Arjun Parker, who had flown in from the United States with his crew. The film was a kaleidoscope of candid shots: from congregation devotees attending discourses in the temple, dancing in kirtan, feasting on the holy *prasadam*, to monks performing temple services, studying *shastras*, lecturing to the congregation, and enjoying themselves in the ashram and temple premises during spare hours. Weaving those footages together into a smooth, intelligible, and inspiring narrative were interviews of leaders who had contributed to the success of the community and also of regular members and newcomers. Arjun Parker had named the documentary *The Simple Temple*. The hour-long film was an instant hit in the ISKCON world, and the temple, along with the ashram, became a role model for emulation all across the globe.

But by 2016, the "simple ashram" had grown complex. Long story short, a lot of junior monks were unhappy with the way they were managed by their seniors. One couldn't put a finger on which party was at fault. Typical issues of a corporate workplace had ironically found their way into an ashram.

In January of 2017, Radhanath Swami called a plenary meeting of all the resident monks to address the issue. His opening lines were epochal: "Ours is no longer a simple temple." That was no news for the insiders, but to see him declare that openly was awe-inspiring. He had laboured—for three long decades—to ensure that the ambience at the temple and the adjoining ashram felt homely for the residents and the visitors alike. As regards how to manage a temple, in the documentary, he had made it clear, "They (the monks) want to surrender. You ask them to collect funds, you ask them to distribute spiritual books, you ask them to worship the deities, and they are enlivened to do so. But if there is not that family spirit, if there is not that faith in the management, then it is very difficult to manage a temple." Radhanath Swami had indeed succeeded in creating and maintaining that family spirit for many long years. But now that things were going awry, it required tons of simplicity on his part to admit it. The tendency of most leaders would be to push such issues under the carpet with glib words and masquerade; and to save one's reputation by turning a blind eye. But Radhanath Swami wasn't of that kind. His temple was no longer simple, but he still was. Having acknowledged that there were issues to be addressed, he went about resolving them unabashed. And so, hopes were galore that things would return to how they were before.

To begin with, he held heart-to-heart conversations with dozens of monks, spending several hours inquiring with them, trying to get his head fully around the situation.

A Simple Person Is Unembarrassed to Enquire

If you have a child, you will have plenty of experiences of being tsunami-ed by seemingly trivial questions. This readiness to enquire is a sacred virtue, especially necessary for spirituality. Irrespective of whether we are beginners or veterans on the spiritual path, we will come across concepts and challenges that baffle us. Only if we are simple will we admit our ignorance and shortcomings, and seek clarifications and help. Even Arjuna demonstrated this trait as he was listening to Sri Krishna's teachings on the battlefield of Kurukshetra:

For instance, after explaining Karma Yoga, when Sri Krishna said something that went over Arjuna's head, Arjuna was quick to admit his incomprehension and asked for clarification.

> Lord Sri Krishna, said: I instructed this imperishable science of Karma Yoga to the sun-god, Vivasvan, and Vivasvan instructed it to Manu, the father of mankind, and Manu in turn instructed it to Ikshvaku. (Bhagavad Gita 4.1)

> Arjuna asked: The sun-god Vivasvan is senior by birth to You. How am I to understand that in the beginning You instructed this science to him? (Bhagavad Gita 4.4)

A Simple Person Unequivocally Trusts

Smile at a toddler, and they will return the smile, even if you are a total stranger. Show them a laddu, and they will come and grab it, their eyes still twinkling. However, try these tactics with an adult and you can expect a grimace, a whack, or anything in between.

Children are naturally simple—their thoughts, words, and actions are spontaneously aligned—and therefore, they are wired to see others in the same light. As the saying goes, "the world is a reflection of your own state of consciousness." Kids can't imagine a scenario where a person thinks one way but speaks or acts differently. They naively assume everyone is as straightforward as they are, and so they trust anyone and everyone.

Therefore, they readily consume whatever knowledge is fed to them. Just as with laddus, so also with information. That's one more reason—again connected to simplicity—which explains why they are fast learners.

As I had told you before, our science teacher at school introduced me to the atom and its structure. I remember her discussing an experiment performed by someone named Rutherford in 1911, and a postulation made by some Bohr. The whole class was bored, scribbling down copious notes. We couldn't see the atom, nor its structure. All we could behold were sketches on the blackboard, supposedly representing the atom's innards. Our teacher claimed that all those experiments she described were indeed performed about a century ago and that the atomic theory was verified through the scientific method—rationally and empirically.

In retrospect, I wonder why none of us challenged her claims. "We would like to do those experiments and reach those conclusions ourselves, rather than blindly believing what you say and what the textbook says"—that argument coming from any of the students would have been perfectly reasonable and scientific. But impractical. We couldn't afford the resources—neither the time nor the money—to replicate every single experiment we were taught. Fortunately, we as kids were capable of placing our trust in our teacher and the science textbook. We did enquire for clarifications, but neither doubted what our teacher said, nor what the textbook contained.

This same childlike simplicity is necessary when we are novices in any field, including spirituality. Otherwise, our journey along the spiritual path will be a non-starter. As beginners, we lack a developed consciousness, the spiritual resource—indeed, the lifeblood—necessary to verify supramundane truths. So, for starters, we learn to place our trust in the scriptures and the realisations of the great souls. Arjuna, on the battlefield of Kurukshetra, set the precedent by trusting Sri Krishna's words. He did enquire for clarification, as we discussed earlier, but when Sri Krishna elaborated, Arjuna took him at his word.

> Arjuna had asked: The sun-god Vivasvan is senior by birth to You. How am I to understand that in the beginning You instructed this science to him? (Bhagavad Gita 4.4)

> Lord Sri Krishna replied: Many, many births both you and I have passed. I can remember all of them, but you cannot, O subduer of the enemy! Although I am unborn and My transcendental body never deteriorates, and although I am the Supreme Lord of all living entities and the gods, I still appear in every millennium in My original transcendental form. Whenever and wherever there is a decline in religious practice, O descendant of Bharata, and a predominant rise of irreligion—at that time I descend Myself. To deliver the pious and to annihilate the miscreants, as well as to reestablish the principles of

religion, I Myself appear, millennium after millennium. One who knows the transcendental nature of My appearance and activities does not, upon leaving the body, take birth again in this material world, but attains My eternal abode. O Arjuna… There is no work that affects Me; nor do I aspire for the fruits of action. One who understands this truth about Me also does not become entangled in the fruitive reactions of work. All the liberated souls in ancient times acted with this understanding of My transcendental nature. Therefore you should perform your duty, following in their footsteps. (Bhagavad Gita 4.5–9, 4.14, 4.15)

A Simple Person Is Happy

We can rely on simple trust not just to learn novel concepts, but also for spiritual advancement and for peace and happiness.

> Ignorant and faithless persons who doubt the revealed scriptures do not attain God consciousness; they fall down. For the doubting soul, there is happiness neither in this world nor in the next. (Bhagavad Gita 4.40)

Back in the day, around the same time as *The Simple Temple* was filmed, I was a student at IIT Bombay and visited Sri Sri Radhagopinath Temple during weekends. I even stayed at the adjoining ashram during vacations. The monks there were the happiest people I had ever met. Sure enough, it was their simplicity that I was taken with—more than any other aspect of their personalities. Their thoughts could be heard through their words and seen in their actions. The monks led a transparent and carefree life, and staying with them was a welcome relief from the diplomatic and complex world outside. That's how I was inspired to eventually join the ashram in 2004 after completing my graduation and postgraduation.

For most people in this world, family is where they exhibit their natural self, and the office is where they put on a different face. People resort to diplomacy at the workplace amid their untrustworthy bosses but retain their simplicity at home with their trustworthy kin. As a result, work life brings stress and anxiety, while family life offsets it by offering a relaxed, carefree, and happy lifestyle. However, life is unbearable for those unfortunate souls who can't even trust family members and can't afford to be simple even at home. For them, there's no respite from stress—neither at the office nor at home. And with such cases increasing in the new world, the graph of unhappiness is steeply on the rise.

For the monks at Radhagopinath Ashram, their home and office were the same place. Both the junior monks and the seniors who managed them lived in the same premises. Notwithstanding, when I joined the ashram in 2004, I couldn't detect a whiff of diplomacy there. Everybody—from the oldies down to the rookies—enjoyed familial loving dealings with each other, even as their days were packed with services that demanded the efficiency of any corporate workplace. The reason was simple—the junior monks trusted their seniors and vice versa.

But then, things started to go sideways after 2010. The trigger was the Swami's increasing responsibilities in the United States. When he became less available in the Mumbai Ashram, what resulted was a domino effect:

The Swami's shoes were too big to fill for anyone around; even the most senior monks found it difficult to deliver the same quantum of spiritual inspiration to the ashram residents as the Swami. Consequently, the monks felt less motivated to serve. The management body found itself struggling to get things done and keep the temple running. Reluctantly, they resorted to the arm-twisting and diplomatic tactics typical of a corporate setup. But it didn't work, for unlike in corporations, these monk-turned-managers had neither carrots nor sticks to straighten out their subordinates. What perks, benefits, or punishments could galvanise into action a group of volunteers who had renounced lucrative careers—as engineers, doctors, lawyers, corporate consultants, and the like! The management of the temple was up against the wall for sure, but a severe fallout of their expediency was that the ashram lost its simplicity. And with it, its carefree ambience. The juniors no longer trusted their seniors, especially those who acted as their managers. Stress and anxiety became palpable. Life at the monastery was now like living out one's life at an office—with all the accompanying diplomacy and duplicity—all through the day and all through the night, week after week, and month after month. A serious aftermath of the situation was that the monks started to struggle with mindfulness during their morning meditation routine.

A Simple Person Is Mindful

Have you ever witnessed a child lost in their new toy? Children have a phenomenal capacity to align their entire being with their thoughts. This ability, born of their simplicity, is what mindfulness is all about. Therefore, for one striving to be simple, mindfulness is much easier to practise. Needless to say, mindfulness forms the backbone of meditation.

> Those interested in achieving self-realisation through control of the mind and senses, mindfully offer the functions of all the senses, and of the life breath, as oblations into the fire of the mind which is rapt in meditation. (Bhagavad Gita 4.27)

Returning to our ashram's story, when the monks lost their simplicity, their mindfulness also began to wane. Their daily meditation became less effective, and their spiritual growth stalled. Ashram life, which had already grown stressful due to diplomacy and duplicity, now became unbearable for many, leading to an unprecedented exodus of monks from the monastery.

So, in 2017, when Radhanath Swami assessed the ashram's situation through extensive interviews with dozens of monks, he came up with a solution. He set up a board that consisted of the most senior monks of the ashram. It was called the Leadership Council and was to act as a caregiving body. These veterans were to act as an inspiring force for the ashram residents, to make them feel at home. Though none of these leaders could individually fill the void left by the Swami's absence, they could still prove a force of nature if they worked conjointly. Crucially, these council members would hold no managerial responsibilities, making them all the more trustworthy in the eyes of the juniors who had lost all faith in the management.

Five years later, now in 2022, is the situation any better? An honest answer would be this: the ashram has definitely emerged from the tangles, but it remains a work-in-progress. For trust, once broken, is incredibly difficult to restore.

If you ask for my take on the entire story, I believe that the onus of rebuilding a simple temple lies as much upon us subordinates as on those who are leading us. Unless we educate ourselves on the importance of having a simple heart and make our best effort to cultivate it, the efforts of our leaders will fall short, no matter how hard they work.

16

TAP THE POWER OF YOUR INTELLIGENCE
Analysing Intelligence

On July 6, 1994, *Forrest Gump* was released in cinemas and became a phenomenon. It won six Oscars, became the fourth highest-grossing film up to that point, and was acclaimed as a cultural touchstone. Nonetheless, it also attracted an avalanche of backlash. In 2014, even 20 years later, CNN called the film "surprisingly polarizing".

For those who haven't watched it, the film is about a simpleton by the name of Forrest Gump and his epic saga of success. Gump wins the Congressional Medal of Honor for his war efforts in Vietnam, becomes a champion of football and ping-pong, gets fabulously wealthy, starts a fitness movement, and ends up having an audience with three American presidents—Johnson, Kennedy, and Nixon. According to Sam Wineburg, a professor of history at Stanford University who has co-authored academic papers about the film's influence, those who loved it viewed it as a "celebration of American goodness and innocence."

Sure enough, every triumph of Gump can be chalked up to his simple and innocent disposition. Take, for instance, his success with ping-pong. In the film, this is how Gump is introduced to the game: "no matter what happens, never ever take your eye off the ball." For Gump, fixing his vision on the bouncing ball is a walk in the park; being simple, he is naturally mindful and focused. He plays his way into the All-American Ping-Pong Team and becomes a national celebrity.

Later in life, when Forrest Gump suffers a heartbreak at the hands of his childhood sweetheart, he embarks on a cross-country marathon. Unwittingly, he attracts public attention and features on the cover page of every magazine worth its salt. At the end of it all, the unassuming Gump muses: "My mama always said, 'You got to put the past behind you before you can move on.' And I think that's what my running was all about." Again, underpinning his rise to fame was his simple trust in the words of his mother.

And what about the windfall that he makes through founding the Bubba-Gump Shrimp Corporation? Once more, you have to hand it to Gump's simplicity. He had promised his deceased friend Bubba about starting a shrimp business, and all he had done was—align his actions with the word that he had given. That he made a killing in the process was just a spin-off.

"*Forrest Gump* touches people with its sweeping story about a gentle soul..." summarised a *Los Angeles Times* article published in 2019.

But then, what's in this "sweeping story" that attracts detractors? "One of the main complaints about the film is that it appears to be anti-intellectual... The film seems to argue that ignorance really is bliss," explained the same *LA Times* article. "This no-nothing white man becomes a war hero and a wealthy man simply by chugging along, participating in a country that dictates his every move. He never comprehends racism or the complexities of Vietnam," noted a write-up that appeared on the film-review website *Indiewire*.

Most people disparage simplicity as synonymous with stupidity, a mental state wherein the faculty for doubting is dysfunctional. At first glance, that seems right. And with Forrest Gump, that's spot on. With a below-average IQ of 75, he is clearly out of his depth to doubt his country's policies or his society's mores.

So yes, intellectually challenged people are naturally simple. But is the converse true? Are all simple people necessarily intellectually challenged?

The answer is a resounding NO. The simplicity exemplified by Arjuna in the Bhagavad Gita, for instance, in no way alludes to a low IQ. Arjuna was a brilliant warrior capable of doubting. But all the same, he chose to offset his shrewdness with simplicity, knowing well the advantages of a simple disposition.

Balancing Shrewdness with Simplicity

According to the Vedas, *samshaya*, the faculty for doubting, is a characteristic of *buddhi*, intelligence; nonetheless, it's only one of many. When an intelligent person like Arjuna finds himself under the grip of samshaya, it's just the first domino that has fallen. He quickly follows up that samshaya with *viparyasa*, an analysis of whether his suspicion holds any water. And finally, he reaches *nischaya*, a conclusion, which could be either that the doubt was valid or that it was invalid. If invalid, he brushes it aside; if valid, he takes necessary action. Regardless, at the end of the line, he rewinds the mind to be simple once again.

In essence, viparyasa and nischaya should ensure that the powder keg of samshaya, once ignited, gets burnt up completely. One should be adept at juggling the three elements of intelligence to ensure that simplicity is one's norm and instances of suspicion are mere blips. How to go about this balancing act is demonstrated by the following story from the life of the founder of the Bajaj Group, Jamnalal Bajaj, whose entire life was a tightrope walk between shrewdness and simplicity.

One of Bajaj's relatives once borrowed money from him. Despite Bajaj's insistence that it be regarded as a gift, the borrower was adamant that it be documented as a loan. But when not a paisa was returned even after three years of the transaction, Bajaj grew dubious of his relative's attitude (samshaya). He analysed the situation (viparyasa) and came to a conclusion (nishchaya). In his own words, "We must always differentiate between friendship and business. My relative's conduct was wholly unbusiness-like and I wanted to teach him a lesson." Bajaj promptly filed a lawsuit for the recovery of the amount, and as he had foreseen, the relative stormed at his doorstep, fretting and fuming. But Bajaj remained unfettered, for he knew exactly what he was doing: "If I had not gone to court, it would have meant I was afraid of his abuses. I did not want such an impression to be created." Bajaj successfully obtained a decree against his relative, but anticlimactically didn't have it executed. "I never wanted to persecute him and so I wrote off the amount," he later explained.

After describing this episode in the book *Jamnalal Bajaj: A Brief Study of his Life and Character*, author T. V. Parvate concludes, "Even after this incident, Jamnalal behaved like a friend with this relative." Put differently, Jamnalal Bajaj returned to his "default setting" of simplicity, after having completed the cycle of samshaya, viparyasa and nishchaya, as the situation at hand had demanded.

Among the 15 principles which Bajaj scrupulously adhered to as a businessman, the very first one was, "Do not affix your signature on any paper before you have read it." There was another one which said, "Before you stand surety for any person, know him well." While these principles alluded to him being a shrewd businessperson, there were others that pointed to his simple and straightforward disposition. For instance, "Always be clean, truthful, and stainless in your business affairs... Never fight shy of plain speaking."

Arjuna's Moments of Doubt as He Listens to the Bhagavad Gita

The flow of the Gita was intercepted whenever Arjuna found himself swayed by intelligent doubts. Take, for example, the following question that he asks:

Arjuna queried: "O Krishna, what are the symptoms of one whose consciousness is merged in transcendence? How does he speak, and what is his language? How does he sit, and how does he walk?" (Bhagavad Gita 2.54)

Being shrewd and thoughtful, Arjuna was bound to doubt (samshaya) any stranger who professed transcendence. The answers to the above questions would assist him in analysing (viparyasa) and reaching a conclusion (nischaya) regarding the authenticity of such a claim.

In response to Arjuna's query, Sri Krishna presents a series of criteria. Here are a few examples:

One who is not disturbed in mind even amidst the threefold miseries or elated when there is happiness, and who is free from attachment, fear, and anger, is called a sage of steady mind. (Bhagavad Gita 2.56)

One who is able to withdraw the senses from sense objects, as the tortoise draws its limbs within the shell, is firmly fixed in perfect consciousness. (Bhagavad Gita 2.58)

One who restrains the senses, keeping them under full control, and fixes the consciousness upon Me, is known as a person of steady intelligence. (Bhagavad Gita 2.61)

At other places in the Gita, Sri Krishna proactively addresses any misgivings that may arise in Arjuna's intelligence. For instance, Sri Krishna dispels doubts concerning the authenticity of Karma Yoga before Arjuna even raises them:

This supreme science of Karma Yoga was received through parampara, and the saintly kings understood it in that way. (Bhagavad Gita 4.2)

A *parampara*, being the rough Vedic equivalent of a modern-day university, ensures the reliability of knowledge received through it. It consists of teachers who impart spiritual knowledge that has been handed down since ancient times through an unbroken lineage. Just as research work by professors keeps the knowledge in a university up-to-date, in a parampara, the realisations of these spiritual teachers keep the ancient wisdom relevant in our ever-changing world. The sacred knowledge base is safeguarded against interference through strict scrutiny; not a modicum of information can be included—or excluded—arbitrarily. While in a university it's a board of directors who are the watchdogs, in a parampara, it's a band of saints who do the patrolling.

The parallels between a university and a parampara extend further. Just as modern education is consummated by submitting to a university professor as your guide, who oversees your research project, Vedic education is complete only when you accept a guru in parampara, under whose guidance you trek the terrain towards higher realisations.

The Bhagavad Gita itself can be seen as a dialogue between the guru Sri Krishna and his disciple Arjuna. In fact, the duo were the trailblazers of a new parampara.

> The ancient parampara that taught Karma Yoga to the saintly kings got decimated over time, and that science now appears to be lost. Today it is retold by Me to you because you are My devotee as well as My friend and can therefore understand its transcendental mystery. (Bhagavad Gita 4.2,3)

The Gita Respects Your Intelligence

There's not a single instance in the Bhagavad Gita where Sri Krishna berates Arjuna for interrupting him with doubts. From the word go, Sri Krishna acknowledged that he was speaking to an intelligent person—and through him, to all intellectuals for all time to come.

"In the morning I bathe my intellect in the stupendous and cosmogonal philosophy of the Bhagavad Gita in comparison with which our modern world and its literature seem puny and trivial," said the American philosopher Henry David Thoreau.

And in Sri Krishna's own words,

> I declare that one who studies this sacred conversation of ours (the Bhagavad Gita) worships Me by his or her intelligence. (Bhagavad Gita 18.70)

17

TAP THE GURU'S WISDOM
Through Submission, Inquiry, and Service

In 1985, New Zealand's rugby team, all set to visit South Africa for a series, cancelled its tour as a mark of protest against apartheid. The African National Congress (ANC), the leading political wing of the black South Africans, had prevailed upon the New Zealand rugby board.

The South African blacks viewed rugby as a white man's sport and detested it. Conversely, for extremist white racists, the game was their secular religion, a focus for their zealotry. The Springboks, South Africa's national team, had earned the reputation of being one of the best teams in the world. This made rugby the one arena where white South Africa could hold its head high on the world stage, despite the scarring presence of apartheid. The rugby frenzy also served as an opiate that kept the non-racist, liberal-minded whites blissfully ignorant of the injustices against the blacks. By denying white South Africa international rugby, the ANC achieved two significant objectives: it exerted a powerful political influence on the international level and awakened white liberals to the reality of racial injustices at home.

At first glance, the campaign against South African rugby appeared a blunt fang among the ANC's snarling array of offensives against the government. These offensives included actions through armed militias, domestic trade unions, international economic sanctions, and diplomatic isolation, among others. However, appearances can be deceptive. Rugby arguably held the most venom. A workers' strike, or even a bomb, would affect a small group. But ostracising the Springboks from international rugby "affected all of them, every white male, every household in a sports-mad country whose main source of pride regarding the rest of the world was its sports prowess," as one of the ANC members put it.

Surprisingly, by 1992, the same ANC had grown effervescently in favour of the Springboks playing on the international stage again. What had changed the tide in those interim seven years? Had the ANC's think tank softened, or had the political party that claimed to represent the oppressed blacks sold its loyalty to the well-heeled whites?

Or, had they repositioned themselves to keep pace with the changing political landscape?

In 1992, black South Africa was beginning to find its place in the sun. The government had agreed to an all-race election, having succumbed to a combination of internal revolution and international pressure. Meanwhile, the white populace—both liberals and extremists—were gripped by fear. Among them were government bureaucrats who feared for their jobs, small businessmen who feared for their shops, farmers who feared for their land. They all feared for their flag, anthem, language, schools, Dutch Reformed Church, and their rugby. Everything could be taken from them if the blacks came to power, which seemed inevitable with an all-race election on the horizon. On top of all this, they feared retribution for decades of oppression.

Amid this tense milieu, the liberals trusted that their politicians would negotiate a compromise with the ANC. The extremists, however, were sceptical and ready to fight. These white tigers, facing both fear and desperation, were poised to pounce in a last-ditch effort at self-preservation. The ANC realised that the need of the hour was to reassure and placate them. The simplest and surest way of doing that was to return their former international rugby status. Through this gesture, the ANC would also signal to the white racists that, if they were willing to cooperate, the rest of the world wouldn't see them as pariahs anymore.

Previously, the ANC had used rugby as a tool to gain political leverage. Now, having achieved that, the sport would be repurposed to reassure the white extremists and create a democracy where all races could coexist peacefully.

But this stratagem would have been a non-starter had the ANC not been guided by Nelson Mandela, arguably the greatest political guru of modern history. His twenty-seven years and six months in prison were akin to a spiritualist's retreat into the wild to unearth profound truths, except that Mandela's explorations were on the political front. It was during his imprisonment that he concluded that the only way to defeat the white tiger was by taming it. He also recognised the political power of sport. Even before his release from prison in 1990, Mandela was the de facto political guru of black South Africa. It was universally acknowledged that he had a higher vision, one which eluded the general populace.

Spirituality is often singled out as the only field that demands an attitude of submission. However, Mandela's years of leadership after his release, during which he steered his nation away from the brink of civil war and towards peace and prosperity, prove otherwise. There were times during his tenure when his supporters had to capitulate to his directives, trusting in his vast political wisdom. In the end, their faith was rewarded.

For instance, they were eventually rewarded for playing along with him—oftentimes against their better judgement—during the step-by-step drama leading up to the 1995 Rugby World Cup finals.

Submission—the First Step

When in 1992, the Springboks were given the green light to play international matches once again, a precondition was put forth by the ANC: henceforward, fans wouldn't use rugby matches as a political platform to promote "apartheid symbols". However, in the very first tournament against New Zealand, the rowdy white crowd defiantly violated these conditions, leaving the ANC leadership feeling betrayed. Despite this, Mandela persisted, arguing that rugby should not be taken away from the whites; instead, the game should be used as an instrument to win them over. And the ANC submitted to his will. They continued to trust him, even as he gave the whites the best, biggest, and least-deserved gift—the 1995 Rugby World Cup Tournament. Not just the chance to participate in it, but also the opportunity to host it.

The ANC's submission to Mandela went through the litmus test on June 25, 1993, a day before the Springboks were to kick-start their preparation for the World Cup by playing against France. At the World Trade Centre in Johannesburg, the ANC was holding a meeting with government delegates to determine the course of the nation after the all-race election, when 3,000 white extremists, every one of them armed to the teeth, stormed the building. No major casualties ensued, but the attackers made it clear that they were dead set against the black man finding his feet. The ANC's reflexive move would have been a counterattack—by pulling the rug from under the white man's feet through cancelling the SA-France rugby match scheduled for the next day—had Mandela not intervened. Mandela argued that rugby could still be used to entice the white liberal—if not the white extremist—to bring him around to support the future black government. The same opiate that once kept the white liberal oblivious to the injustices against the blacks would now be used to numb his pain when power and undue privileges would be taken from him. If rugby were also snatched away, there was the risk of the liberal waking from his political torpor and joining the extremist camp. Yet again, the ANC submitted to Mandela's wisdom, and the SA-France match happened in Durban the next day, as per schedule.

But as history would prove, rugby—and especially the World Cup—would play a bigger role than merely an analgesic. It held the potential to be the elixir for national integration. And it was Mandela who again deployed the sport in accordance with this potential.

Following the elections, when he was sworn in as the president on May 10, 1994, Mandela took charge of a nation that was split historically, culturally, racially, and in every conceivable way. There was no precedent of a country with such multiple fractures ever fully healing. The simmering hostilities between the races had come to a boil in the form of open defiance and violence during the recent polls that had brought him to power. Almost half the white extremists had abstained from voting. On top of that, some of them had planted bombs in black localities a week before the elections, killing 21 and seriously injuring hundreds. The priority task ahead of Mandela was to unify a fragile South Africa, and with that in mind, he flew to meet the Springboks, who were in training sessions, preparing for the World Cup. "You now have the opportunity of serving South Africa and uniting our people," he told them. The subtext of the meeting was clear: the Springboks were being called upon to bear the additional responsibility of playing for a political cause. Hitherto, rugby was used by the ANC, a body that represented the blacks, to reach out to the whites; henceforth, the game should be used by the Springboks, a team that de facto represented the whites, to win over the resentful black population. And the Springboks were more than willing to play that role. The president had stuck out his neck to offer them international rugby, and now it was their turn to reciprocate, by submitting to his will.

They began by adopting the "One Team, One Country" slogan, which encapsulated their new message that the Springboks were now the team of black South Africa as much as they were of the whites'. The victory of South African rugby would be shared by all, blacks and whites alike. They visited black neighbourhoods, chatted and played with the children there, teaching them rugby, and introducing them to the new "national game". They even included a coloured player in their squad.

Mandela had told the Springboks when he met them, "Just remember, all of us, black and white, are behind you." Now, while the Springboks did their best to cosy up to the blacks, Mandela set out to convince the blacks to mend fences with the Springboks. The ANC giving their nod to the rugby team had definitely been a milestone, but the black masses lending their weight to the Springboks was the holy grail he sought.

When he put on a Springboks cap during an all-black rally, Mandela realised what an onerous task lay ahead of him: he was booed by the very people he had sacrificed his life for. But he held on to his character and refused to take any offence. After all, this was an area where "apartheid left communities in conditions that defy description," as Mandela would explain later. Notwithstanding, the dismal past was no excuse for denying a distinguished future. He called upon the wiser selves of his audience. "Amongst you are leaders. Don't be shortsighted, don't be emotional. Nation-building means that we have to pay a price, in the same way that the whites have to pay a price. For them to open sports to black people: they are paying a price; for us to say we must now embrace the rugby team is paying a price. That's what we should do." As the booing slowly subsided, he continued, "I want leaders amongst you, men and women, to stand up and promote this idea." As always, Mandela eventually prevailed, and they submitted to his will.

Inquiry—the Second Step

Submission to a guru is substantiated through seeking guidance from him, especially before making decisions on critical issues. Mandela taught this lesson to the ANC's leadership in no uncertain terms during a meeting held in the run-up to the all-race elections. The ANC chiefs had gathered to discuss what the future national anthem would be, and before they could start, Mandela had to exit the meeting to attend an important phone call. By the time he returned, the decision was already made. "Die Stem", the old anthem the whites bellowed out, would be replaced by "Nkosi Sikelel' iAfrika", the hitherto unofficial anthem that had galvanised the blacks during their struggle against their oppressors.

Mandela could foresee the far-reaching consequences this ruling would have on all facets of a white man's life. Take alone the context of rugby. The change in national anthem meant that the almost all-white Springboks would now have to sing "Nkosi Sikelel' iAfrika" before playing any match during the 1995 Rugby World Cup. Most of them didn't understand its meaning, and couldn't spell many of its words. And for crying out loud, the chances of it stirring their emotions and stoking their inspiration stood at one in a million.

Mandela could relate to the impending heartbreak of the white folks if their "Die Stem" were taken away. "Well, I am sorry. I don't want to be rude," he addressed his ANC colleagues after hearing them out. "But... I think I should express myself on this motion. I never thought seasoned people such as yourselves would take a decision of such magnitude on such an important matter without even waiting for the president of your organization... This song that you treat so easily holds the emotions of many people whom you don't represent yet. With the stroke of a pen, you would take a decision to destroy the very—the only—basis that we are building upon: reconciliation."

The ANC had submitted to him as their guru but hadn't bothered to inquire from him regarding a critical issue. Having realised their folly, they caved in and now asked for his opinion. Mandela proposed that both "Die Stem" and "Nkosi Sikelel' iAfrika" be part of the national anthem, and both be sung one after the other at all official ceremonies. The idea was unanimously approved.

The ANC had missed a step but nonetheless had recanted. The Springboks, on the other hand, were perfectly attuned to their newly found political guru's mood right from the word go. They were guided by his heart, without him having to speak out its contents aloud. They were already an integral part of his mission-impossible, of bringing black and white South Africa closer. No sooner did they get a drift of the new national anthem, than they reached out to someone who was an expert in Xhosa, the language in which "Nkosi Sikelel' iAfrika" was composed. They learnt from her how to sing it, and followed that up through enthusiastic rehearsals, to ensure that when they sang the "Nkosi Sikelel' iAfrika" on the field before kick-starting a match, they belted it out with full gusto, so that the blacks would be convinced that the Springboks were indeed standing by their "One Team, One Country" slogan.

Service—the Third Step

During the lead-up to the World Cup, when Mandela had flown to see the Springboks, captain François Pienaar had given a farewell speech to the President towards the conclusion of the impromptu meeting. Addressing his team, he had said, "There's one guy that now we understand we have to play for, and that's the president." Mandela had given them a purpose—to play for the entire nation—and playing for him meant playing for national integration.

All the upsides of a purpose-driven mindset rallied behind the Springboks. In the words of Du Plessis, the manager of the team, "There was a cause-and-effect connection between the Mandela factor and our performance in the field. It was cause and effect on a thousand fronts. In players overcoming the pain barrier, in a superior desire to win, in luck going your way because you make your own luck, in all kinds of tiny details that together or separately mark the difference between winning and losing."

As they elbowed their way up through the lower stages of the tournament, there was a unique observation made by the Springboks. In the words of Hennie le Roux, a Springbok, "We could see the country really was uniting around us, but it was through winning that we would make that bond stronger. The better we did on the pitch, the wider the ripple effect off it." When the team drove back and forth between their hotel and the training camps, the roads would be lined with cheering fans. And the proportion of black supporters increased with every new feather on the Springboks' cap. And that, in turn, would inspire the team to forge yet another victory. South Africa had been thrust into an upward spiral by Mandela's wizardry.

But the semi-finals against France threatened to obstruct this whirlwind of national unification that was set into motion.

The match was to be held at Durban, but a downpour had left the field waterlogged. If the game were cancelled, World Cup rules decreed that France would be declared the winner. The heavyweight white giants of the South African rugby team had brought the team thus far, and now the baton of service to the president and to the nation was taken over from them by black ladies with mops and buckets. Military helicopters might have played their role in fanning the field from above, but the women's battalion's "heroic labours persuaded the referee to let the game proceed," according to John Carlin, the author of *Playing the Enemy: Nelson Mandela and the Game That Made a Nation*. The game against France was "a battle of wills, more than anything else," according to Du Plessis. "It was the game in which we really felt that Mandela magic had an impact on us on the field of play."

And that magic would overflow the field and spill over onto the stands when South Africa played New Zealand in the finals.

The Miracle of Accepting a Guru through Submission, Inquiry, and Service

A cardinal couplet of the Bhagavad Gita is where Lord Sri Krishna first stresses the importance of accepting a guru, and then explains the miraculous effect of doing so.

> One can progress on the spiritual path by accepting a guru. By inquiring submissively and by rendering service. The self-realized souls can guide a disciple because they have seen the truth. (Bhagavad Gita 4.34)

> Thus being guided by a guru, you will begin to see all living beings as spiritual, as parts of the Supreme, or, in other words, as belonging to Me. You will never fall again into the illusion of viewing them in terms of their disparate material identities. (Bhagavad Gita 4.35)

Among the above verses, the first one may sound servile, and the second unworldly. Notwithstanding, the principles they state apply not just to spirituality, but to many other fields including politics. The Springboks had accepted Mandela as their political guru, through submission, inquiry, and service, whether or not they consciously saw him in that light; so had the ANC, and so had black South Africa as a whole. And the effect of that was self-evident. All the people of the nation were beginning to see each other as South Africans—first and foremost—regardless of superficial differences in terms of race, religion, or tribe.

"The Rugby World Cup has led to a spectacular upsurge of national reconciliation among all races in South Africa, researchers and social scientists reported this week," noted a prominent Cape Town newspaper on the morning of June 24, 1995. But the extent of South Africa's progress in its journey towards unification remained to be seen during the Finals scheduled to be played that very afternoon—when the Springboks clashed against New Zealand in Johannesburg, a city that was a hotbed of white extremism. Among the 65,000 spectators expected at the Ellis Park Stadium, many would be the very people who stormed the World Trade Centre exactly two years ago, vowing to keep the black man wrapped around their little fingers forever. How would they react to "Nkosi Sikelele' iAfrika" when sung before the start of the match? Would they jeer at it? Would they unfurl the old orange, blue, and white South African flag that symbolised apartheid? Meanwhile, the question that troubled the PPU, Presidential Protection Unit, was far more sinister: would the extremist white crowd attempt to assassinate Nelson Mandela as he walked to the middle of the ground to greet the players before the beginning of the match?

The answer came when Mandela actually stepped on the grass of Ellis Park five minutes before kickoff. The spectators—95 percent of them white extremists—were stunned when they saw him donned neck-to-toe in a Springbok jersey and sporting a Springbok cap. Their immediate reaction was dead silence, the silence that comes before the storm. Then a chant emerged, slow at first, then rising in volume and intensity. "Nel-son! Nel-son! Nel-son!"

The entire stadium was swept by the storm of cheers for the President.

As the Springboks captain François Pienaar would later recollect, "It was a moment of magic, a moment of wonder. It was the moment I realised that there really was a chance this country could work. This man was showing that he could forgive, totally, and now they—white South Africa, rugby white South Africa—they showed in that response to him that they too wanted to give back, and that was how they did it, chanting, 'Nelson! Nelson!' It was awe-inspiring. It was fairytale stuff!"

For an ANC leader who was watching this drama on television, this was the moment when he clearly understood that the liberation struggle of the blacks was not so much about freedom from bondage, "but more so, it was about liberating white people from fear. And there it was. 'Nelson! Nelson! Nelson!' Fear melting away."

It felt as if the entire nation was tasting victory—the victory of national unification—even before the match had started. For, the euphoria of the moment didn't just inundate the 62,000 South Africans within the stadium, but also the 43 million glued to the live telecast on TV. But the Springboks knew—going by their experience in the World Cup so far—that in order to immortalise this moment of national integration, they had to win at all costs. It didn't matter that they were up against the New Zealanders—whom the London Daily Telegraph had called—"the most astonishingly talented" rugby side anyone could remember.

Even as rugby pundits had all along predicted a one-sided game, with New Zealand dominating it throughout, the Springboks fought back tooth and nail, driven by patriotism that Mandela had infused in them. They dragged the match into extra time, and eventually emerged victorious.

No sooner had the waves of victory swamped the stadium than the chants of "Nel-son! Nel-son!" resumed, louder than ever before, more visceral, accompanied with scenes of people crying and hugging each other.

During the first phase of "Nel-son!" chants, before the match began, the PPU's cold-vision had caught sight of a few old South African flags waving at the right corner of the stadium. Now in the second phase, all of them had disappeared, being replaced by the new South African flags. Even in that section of the crowd, people could be seen cheering the President with tears of joy.

Meanwhile, in South African homes, white matrons were shedding generations of prejudice and restraint by hugging their black housekeepers and dancing with them.

Guided by their political guru Nelson Mandela, the Springboks had used their profession—as rugby players—for the higher purpose of serving the nation. In much the same way as a spiritual guru guides a disciple to use his or her prescribed duties for the highest purpose of serving God—which is what Karma Yoga is all about.

The Springboks had successfully united a fragmented South Africa without having to resort to sit-ins, campaigns, protests, or the blood-and-guts that usually buttresses a political movement of such magnitude. They had achieved the impossible using as preposterous a medium as sport. In the same vein, even in Karma Yoga it doesn't matter how materialistic the talents and resources at your disposal may seem; a bona fide guru coming in parampara can give you the insight to use it all for your spiritual progress—provided that you are willing to submit, inquire, and serve.

18

REACHING THE SUMMIT OF KARMA YOGA
The Awakening of Jnana

In 1997, Rafael Nadal, then just an 11-year-old, won the Spanish under-12s national tennis championship. His whole family was busy celebrating except for his uncle and coach, Toni, who intended to bring him back down to earth. Toni phoned up the Spanish Tennis Federation posing as a journalist and retrieved the list of winners from the preceding 25 years. Then he read their names out loud and asked Nadal if he had ever heard of any of them. "There were just five who had reached a decent level as professionals, whose names meant something to me," recalls Rafa in his biography. "Toni was triumphant. 'You see? The chances of you making it as a pro are one in five. So, Rafael, don't get too excited about today's victory. There's still a long, hard road ahead. And it all depends on you.'"

In 2010, a 24-year-old Rafa won the US Open, and in doing so, became the first player to win consecutive Grand

Slam titles on clay, grass, and hard courts in a calendar year. He also became the seventh player in history to win four Grand Slams and the youngest to do so in the Open era. This time it wasn't just his family adulating him, but the entire world of tennis.

Apparently, for Uncle Toni, his nephew still had "a long, hard road ahead" and nothing to "get too excited about." And even Nadal seemed to share the same viewpoint; just two days after he lifted the US Open trophy, he was back on court hitting balls with Uncle Toni in their hometown in Spain.

In her book, *Grit*, author Angela Duckworth lays down two equations that encapsulate Rafa's relentless training regime.

Talent x Effort = Skill

Skill x Effort = Achievement

She elaborates: "What this theory says is that when you consider individuals in identical circumstances, what each achieves depends on just two things, talent and effort. Talent... absolutely matters. But effort factors into the calculations *twice*, not once. Effort builds skill. At the very same time, effort makes skill productive."

Applying this theory to Rafa's context, he was a talented kid at the age of 11, but it was Toni who groomed him to take the "long, hard road" of effort to build skills. And at 24, when his skills were well-developed, the time was ripe to put in more effort to make those skills fully productive.

Mathematising Karma Yoga

As previously discussed, the "efforts" you invest in yajnas—though they may be with materialistic motives—equip you with the "skill" to serve God with a purpose-driven attitude. As you continue with those efforts of yajna performances—now with a purposeful state of mind—you reach the "achievement" of *Jnana*. Jnana is a stage of spiritual perfection wherein the spiritual truth, once theoretical, becomes realised. That you are the atma, that your identity is spiritual.

Regarding the role of "talent" on the spiritual path, it suffices to be a human being; a human consciousness inherently possesses the "talent" needed to awaken transcendental realisation within your heart.

After substituting the spiritual equivalents of talent, effort, skill, and achievement into Duckworth's equations, they are transformed as follows:

Human consciousness x Yajnas = Purpose-driven attitude

Purpose-driven attitude x Yajnas = Jnana

As per the Gita, the yajnas in the second equation are superior to those in the first.

> Yajnas aimed at achieving Jnana are superior to Yajnas performed for material gains. Though eventually, all Yajnas culminate in Jnana. (Bhagavad Gita 4.33)

It's noteworthy that yajnas factor into the above calculations twice, not once. Therefore, a spiritual coach will never recommend a decrease in efforts when it comes to yajna performances. Your guru will continue to prescribe you yajnas in accordance with your professional, social, and spiritual status, regardless of how far you have journeyed from the backwater of wants to become purpose-driven to serve God.

Consider the varied yajnas that Sri Krishna lists in the Gita for different categories of people, from the neophytes to the advanced:

> Some yogis perfectly worship the devas by offering different sacrifices to them, and some offer sacrifices in the fire of the Supreme Brahman. (Bhagavad Gita 4.25)

> Some, the unadulterated celibates, sacrifice the hearing process and the senses in the fire of mental control, and others, the regulated householders, sacrifice the objects of the senses in the fire of the senses. (Bhagavad Gita 4.26)

> Having accepted strict vows, some become enlightened by sacrificing their possessions, and others by performing severe austerities, by practicing the yoga of eightfold mysticism, or by studying the Vedas to advance in transcendental knowledge. (Bhagavad Gita 4.28)

> Still others, who are inclined to the process of breath restraint to remain in trance, practise by offering the movement of the outgoing breath into the incoming, and the incoming breath into the outgoing, and thus at last remain in trance, stopping all breathing. Others, curtailing the eating process, offer the outgoing breath into itself as a sacrifice. (Bhagavad Gita 4.29)

The Journey of Karma Yoga Can Often Be Imperceptible

On your journey of Karma Yoga, the trek is usually exciting at the beginning: your enthusiastic incorporation of yajnas into your lifestyle, and your newfound aspiration to do everything you do purposefully, as a service to Sri Krishna. But after that initial flurry of activity, you may start feeling as if you are going nowhere, that your heart remains want-driven no matter how sincere your efforts. It can be likened to a first-time flier's perception that their plane is standing still in mid-air. Even if they peep down the porthole, it doesn't seem that the plane is covering much ground. Yet in reality, it's zipping along at a steady speed of 900 km/hr. A more sombre example would be the stealthy encroachment of old age. You look at yourself in the mirror every morning, and you can hardly notice a difference from one day to the next. Yet in reality, you are ageing every nanosecond.

Your spiritual journey may sometimes feel stagnant, but rest assured that you are moving towards perfection at every moment. Raised in a culture of fast food and instant coffee, we've forgotten the virtue of patience, expecting even in spirituality to see instantaneous results. But such outcomes are rare. More often than not, you can only expect gradual changes.

That's not to say that you will observe a tangible change in your consciousness only when you are perfectly purpose-driven. You will definitely see yourself growing more and more purposeful even as you travel along the spiritual path; only that you should measure your progress after longer stretches of time. Speaking for myself, I first clocked a noticeable change in my consciousness about six months into my spiritual journey. Living in a hostel at the time, one morning as I was sweeping my room, I surprised myself by going the extra mile to avoid harming a few ants that crawled on the floor. "Am I the same person who a few years ago used to burn moths alive as a pastime?" I found myself thinking. That was my moment of tasting spiritual blood. My conviction grew stronger; my spiritual practices deepened; and consequently, the next milestone on my spiritual journey came sooner. That's how it works: the more you experience progress, the more frequently you start experiencing it.

Eventually, a day will come—sooner or later, depending on your sincerity and seriousness—when you start seeing every act of yours as an act of sacrifice.

> Every action of a person situated in Karma Yoga is like a yajna in which the fire, the ghee poured into the fire, the oblations, and the consciousness in which the offerings are made are all spiritual. Therefore, the destination of such a person is also spiritual. (Bhagavad Gita 4.24)

This stage of perfection is called Nishkama Karma Yoga, the term Nishkama literally meaning that your heart is "devoid of wants and desires". And that's when Jnana, or transcendental knowledge, awakens.

Your journey may have begun with a degree of faith, but it culminates in a concrete experience of the reality that you are indeed a spirit soul.

A faithful person who is dedicated to attaining Jnana, and who regulates the senses as per the scriptural injunctions is eligible to reach the Jnana stage of perfection, and having achieved it quickly attains the supreme spiritual peace. (Bhagavad Gita 4.39)

In this world, there is nothing so sublime and pure as Jnana. Such realisation is the mature fruit of all mysticism. And one who has become accomplished in Karma Yoga enjoys these realisations from within in due course of time. (Bhagavad Gita 4.38)

PART V

The Perfection of Karma Yoga

19

THE LIFE OF A KARMA YOGI
An Example from Modern Times

January 26, 2001, was a doomsday in the Kutch district of Gujarat. At 8:46 a.m. IST, an earthquake laid waste to 3,40,000 structures, burying thousands and leaving them either dead or squirming beneath the debris. Millions were left homeless.

When industrialist Arvind Mafatlal arrived at one of the grieving villages, people thronged to him for financial assistance. But he declined to part with even a paisa. The destitute were cast aside. Was this the same legendary philanthropist about whom they had heard for decades?

Mafatlal had famously visited Ranka in Bihar when the village was ravaged by famine in 1967. He was so affected by the poverty and misery that he abstained from consuming even a grain of rice until his relief efforts put the villagers back on their feet. Mafatlal had been by the side of the suffering masses in the same vein for decades, regardless of the natural calamity they faced. And even when nature wasn't unleashing her fury, his finances rushed to prop up free medical camps, hospitals for the poor, educational institutions for the underprivileged, and initiatives for rural development. His philanthropic works had spanned all across the country on an epic scale. Was all of that folklore? Or worse, a publicity stunt by the Mafatlal Group? The villagers now mused.

What they failed to grasp was that Mafatlal's compassion sprung from a sanctified heart, not a sentimental mind. He knew better what they needed than they themselves did. He would surely help them, but not in the way they expected him to. For he had a higher vision. For he, more than a philanthropist, was a Karma Yogi.

A Karma Yogi Sees the World While Firmly Situated in the Identity of Being an Atma

As we discussed in the previous chapter, Jnana is born when you reach the perfection of Karma Yoga. And that's when you clearly realise your spiritual nature, more than ever before.

> A person whose Jnana is awakened, even though engaged in seeing, hearing, touching, smelling, eating, moving about, sleeping, and breathing, always knows within himself that he actually does nothing at all. Because while speaking, evacuating, receiving, or opening or closing his eyes, he always knows that only the material senses are engaged with their objects and that he, the atma, is aloof from them. (Bhagavad Gita 5.8,9)

The effect that Jnana has on your consciousness can be compared to what a woman experiences when a child is born to her.

Let me explain.

As I am typing these words, my niece is contemplating motherhood. Perhaps in preparation, she is asking school friends who are now parents, gathering information from the internet, and I honestly don't know what else. But I can confidently say one thing: she is going to be in for a surprise when a baby actually lands on her lap. For theoretical understanding is much different from realisation when it comes to motherhood. In the words of YouTuber Colleen Ballinger, "I have a whole new perspective on pregnancy and motherhood now that I am experiencing it." From Hollywood, Natalie Wood said after she gave birth to her daughter, "I never knew motherhood could be so truly gratifying until I had Natasha." And from Bollywood, it was Juhi Chawla who exclaimed, "Motherhood has made me a much better person. I see everything from a new perspective—with a sense of wonderment."

This significant shift in a woman's outlook towards motherhood can be attributed to the positive alteration in her brain that naturally follows conception and childbirth. "Grey matter becomes more concentrated. Activity increases in regions that control empathy, anxiety, and social interaction. On the most basic level, these changes, prompted by a flood of hormones during pregnancy and in the postpartum period, help attract a new mother to her baby," reads an article from a 2015 issue of *The Atlantic*.

When Jnana is born, it's more your consciousness than your neurons that undergoes a transformation, a change that's far more radical. The realisations that awaken in you are far-reaching, much more exciting than your theoretical conception of spirituality could ever dream up. The Gita describes this milestone on your spiritual journey with great panache.

> When one is enlightened with Jnana, by which nescience is destroyed, then this realisation reveals everything, as the sun lights up everything in the daytime. (Bhagavad Gita 5.16)

In that light of Jnana, you not only clearly discern your own spiritual nature, but also start seeing everyone around—humans, birds, and beasts—in the same light.

> The enlightened, by virtue of true knowledge, see with equal vision a learned and gentle person, a cow, an elephant, a dog, and one who is considered an outcaste by societal standards. (Bhagavad Gita 5.18)

In other words, you realise that the same atma that animates your body resides in every being, regardless of external distinctions. And with that realisation, you are able to relate to the misery of others viscerally, at a level much deeper than your intellect can ever comprehend.

Empowered by that deep sense of empathy, Arvind Mafatlal instructed his team of engineers and technicians who had accompanied him to the earthquake-hit village in Gujarat, "For this village, make provisions for just two things—drinking water, and a way to protect the honour of the women. Give them a place to bathe in privacy, give them their washrooms in privacy and provide plenty of water. If you have to erect a tower for water, erect it. But nothing else."

Then he addressed the villagers, "Let everyone line up here and tell me what you are best at." When some ladies mentioned they were good at stitching clothes, he provided them fabrics and sewing machines. To a man who identified himself as a carpenter, Mafatlal instructed, "Alright. Go around and check out the trees that have fallen. Collect the logs and bring them here." To those who were masons, he suggested they gather stones and bricks from the debris. Once all requisite raw materials had been collected, Mafatlal said, "Now, build your houses." The villagers set to work and rebuilt their homes.

The new makeshift residences, built from materials salvaged from collapsed structures, were certainly not penthouses. However, on the faces of the villagers, there was now pride and satisfaction; the unspoken statement was— "This is my house. I made it."

In Arvind Mafatlal's biography, *A Life Lived with Grace*, author Mini Chandran Curian concludes this Gujarat episode eloquently,

> Thus, Arvind Mafatlal galvanised everyone around him, shaking them out of the dull, hopeless stupor they had fallen into, and got them working constructively. More importantly, he had helped them regain their sense of self-respect, their honour. In that terrible state of deprivation, the edge of their self-image had lost its defined sharpness. But by the very act of rebuilding their homes, they had, in a sense, taken the first step to rebuilding their lives.

As the saying goes—all's well that ends well. The Gujarat story had a happy ending with the villagers regaining lost hope, but let's not overlook the risk Mafatlal had taken to make it happen—by initially declining their pleas for monetary help. Especially in the wake of an apocalyptic calamity, this bold act could have damaged his reputation. In the heat of the moment, people or the media could have questioned why he was there if his money wasn't.

Mafatlal had the courage to deny monetary help and implement a far-sighted vision instead, because he cared little for his identity as a benevolent philanthropist.

A Karma Yogi, Being Purpose-Driven, Can Judiciously Let Go of Material Identities

Arvind Mafatlal's ability to relinquish material identities underpinned each of his successes, and more strikingly, his finesse in achieving diverse accomplishments. While he catapulted the Mafatlal Group into the top three of India's business landscape, he bolstered its reputation as uncompromisingly ethical; while he applied his keen eye for profit, he ensured he was not harming his employees or customers; while he extended himself to embrace the masses, he did not neglect his family; and while he was a man of the world, he was prepared for the afterworld.

In his role as an industrialist, Mafatlal was significantly ahead of his time. "Even as early as the sixties and seventies, he entered into international joint ventures, and this, at a time when India was still struggling to shed its snake-charmer image," reminisces N. V. Iyer, former senior partner of C. C. Chokshi & Company. "Arvindbhai envisaged that a petrochemical complex could be set up in a newly independent country like India, that an Indian company could work as equal partners with big entities like Shell and Hoechst—that requires remarkable vision." And former technocrat of Hoechst, Dr. Erich Sattler Dornbacher, has plenty to say about Mafatlal: "Oh, he was a visionary... even his dreams were larger than his life!"

Yet Mafatlal relinquished his identity as a big dreamer whenever it conflicted with ethics, an uncommon trait indeed. "History shows that where ethics and economics come in conflict, victory is always with economics," Dr. B. R. Ambedkar once said, and he couldn't have been more right. He also opined that people adhered to ethics, even at the cost of vested interests, only if "there was sufficient force to compel them." For Mafatlal, that "sufficient force" came not from external pressures but from within—from his purpose-driven attitude to serve God. "He saw morality as a way of pleasing God, and hence, uncompromisable," says his son, Hrishikesh. Consequently, his relationships with giant multinationals that bolstered his group were unwaveringly honest and transparent. In this connection, a retired executive of Mafatlal Group, Sharad Ambekar, shares an interesting story: "When I was working on the petrochemical project, I had to meet the Shell executives in London, and was questioned in detail about NOCIL, which was a joint venture between Shell and Mafatlals. They asked me probing questions like how old was Arvindbhai, about his stamina, his health...whether he'd be able to stick to his financial commitments. I gave them a realistic picture, which incorporated both the strengths and weaknesses of the Mafatlal Group. Later, I was wondering whether I had erred in being so honest. But when I told Arvindbhai about the discussions, he was pleased with me."

Mafatlal's adherence to principles wouldn't waver even on the domestic front. For instance, in 1960, he passed up a big and easy money-making opportunity because it was unethical. His management predicted that the share prices of Standard Mills would climb and advised him to buy off its shares through *benami* sources. Mafatlal, however, rejected the idea, stating, "Whatever happens, I will not compromise on my integrity." The share prices did rise, and the Mafatlal Group lost a chance at making a significant gain. But unbeknownst to them, it had also saved itself a world of trouble: later, when the Reserve Bank of India conducted a surprise probe into illegal trading, the group received a clean chit. The bank's governor, H. V. Iyengar, called up Mafatlal and said, "A lot of people would have taken advantage of this situation, but you are remarkable, Arvind; you wouldn't be tempted by money even when it's just a stone's throw away from you."

Not that Mafatlal was averse to money-making. After all, he ventured into petrochemicals, plastics, and rubber chemicals for greater profits, while simultaneously expanding and consolidating his textile business. And he negotiated equal partnerships with giant multinationals in joint ventures for drawing more profits. But he would also relinquish the identity of being a profit-hungry businessman every time it conflicted with the wellbeing of his customers, agents, or employees. Because he saw none of them as objects of exploitation, but as children of God whose interests he had to safeguard. As one of his colleagues put it, "Whenever the history of industrialists in India will be written, he will be remembered as an Industrial Mahatma."

Retired General Manager Pramukh Patel recollects: "We, as the marketing team, couldn't keep pace with the way Arvindbhai's mind raced ahead of the market. He wanted to capture both the domestic and international markets. He was ambitious and far-sighted, but at the same time, the consumer always occupied the top place in his order of things." During the Indo–Pak War of 1971, for instance, the contract for manufacturing army uniforms was given to the Mafatlals. Understandably, amid a war, the army personnel couldn't afford the time to cross-check any shortcomings. However, Mafatlal repeatedly emphasised to his staff that under no circumstances should they deceive the government. Mafatlal was equally concerned about his agents and distributors. "If he felt that the textiles market was not going to do well in the next few months, he would tell us that frankly. It would never bother him that by doing so, the distributors might not lift his goods and that he would suffer a loss," says Vijubhai Kothari, who was a longtime agent. And to his workforce, Mafatlal was like a father. Once while addressing his employees, he expressed, "I can replace a non-functioning machine. But if you are not at peace mentally, or if you are dissatisfied, it can create havoc. I care more for you than my machines. A machine can be replaced, you can't."

A mistake that's not uncommon among socially conscientious people like Mafatlal is to neglect their own kith and kin. Take, for example, Erin Brockovich, an environmental activist for over three decades, who also has a family to care for. Talking about her three children, Brockovich recently admitted to *People* magazine that she "didn't see them often" and "that was tough on them." Mafatlal, on the other hand, never cut corners as a family man. After all, they, too, were God's children, and furthermore, entrusted to him for special care. So, for the sake of his family, he didn't mind setting aside his identity even as a philanthropist.

For example, his wedding gift to one of his grandsons was a honeymoon trip to Europe—all expenses paid and the entire itinerary immaculately chalked out with his Swiss travel agent. But more than lavishness, he showered his family with affection. "There was not a day in my life that I couldn't sit down and talk to him like he was my friend," says Vishad Mafatlal, another of his grandsons. "One thing that really mattered to him was the whole family having dinner together at home. All of us looked forward to it... and even after we were done eating, we would continue to linger around the table for a while until our hands dried up." For one of his granddaughters, her favourite childhood memory is the time spent listening to his beautiful, animated stories of Lord Rama and Hanumanji. "He was the best storyteller ever, who made all the characters in his stories come alive."

Even though Arvind Mafatlal constantly juggled his identities, relinquishing one to adopt another as the situation at hand demanded, deep within, he was the same person singularly driven to serve God. "My father was the same whether he was talking to us, or to his employees, to senior government officials or his foreign associates," says Hrishikesh Mafatlal. "This is why people from all walks of life instinctively felt close to him, they felt valued and respected. He always related to people from his heart, and he was never moody or ill-tempered."

> One who works in devotion, who is a pure soul, and who controls his mind and senses, is dear to everyone, and everyone is dear to him. Though always working, such a man is never entangled. (Bhagavad Gita 5.7)

Having mastered the art of letting go, Mafatlal made the most of opportunities life presented. And whenever misfortunes befell, he dealt with them in the same way—by shedding identities.

On the personal front, when his young son died, he didn't allow the identity of being a loving father to affect his professional commitments. He accepted the loss and returned to work. "I often felt that for him, continuing in business was only so that he could direct the profits into serving his guru and Lord Rama at Chitrakoot," says a close relative of his. Mafatlal's Guru was Ranchoddas Maharaj, who belonged to the Ramanandi disciplic succession, or parampara. And it was Maharaj who inspired him to make Chitrakoot, a holy place connected with Lord Ram, the base for his altruistic activities that spanned across the country.

On the business front, the empire that Mafatlal had solidified over the decades diminished in the 1980s and 90s, primarily due to a textile recession and labour unrest. But he didn't let the identity of being a "loser" consume him. Initiating new enterprises in the areas of plastic processing machinery, electronic components, medical equipment, software, and finance, he soldiered on. Nonetheless, the going was tough, with new competitors entering India post-liberalisation. In the year 2000, the group's flagship company, Mafatlal Industries Limited, was declared sick. Some ridiculed and criticised Mafatlal for the failure, but he never responded with resentment. "He was a man at complete peace with himself..." as his grandson Chaitanya recollects.

> A person who neither rejoices upon achieving something pleasant nor laments upon obtaining something unpleasant, who is self-intelligent, who is unbewildered, and who knows the science of God, is already situated in transcendence. (Bhagavad Gita 5.20)

> One who performs his duty without attachment, surrendering the results unto the Supreme Lord, is unentangled, as the lotus leaf is untouched by water. (Bhagavad Gita 5.10)

And when Mafatlal suffered strokes, in 2005 and 2007, paralysing parts of his ageing body, his enlightened spiritual intelligence interpreted the writing on the wall—it was time to allow the droplets of worldly identities to slide off the lotus leaf of his life. He retired and devoted all his time to spirituality.

"My father left his body on Sunday, October 30, 2011, at Chitrakoot," recalls Hrishikesh Mafatlal. "Just five minutes after the last chapter of the Ram Charit Manas was read out to him, after 17 consecutive days of recitation, he closed his eyes forever. It was as if he had been waiting to hear the last holy word before he left his body."

When one's intelligence, mind, faith, and refuge are all fixed in the Supreme, then one becomes fully cleansed of misgivings through complete knowledge and thus proceeds straight on the path of liberation. (Bhagavad Gita 5.17)

20

EXPERIENCING THE DIVINE IN KARMA YOGA
Through Sankirtana Yajna

On a cloudy July morning in 1998, a gentleman strutted into our classroom at IIT Bombay. His dishevelled grey hair, wrinkled skin, and scholarly look clearly distinguished him as a professor. We freshmen were seated inside, all excited for the very first tutorial of the B.Tech programme to commence. Upon seeing the professor, we quietened. Then, as we rose from our seats to greet the elderly man, he shot back a snigger and, with a wave of his left hand, nonchalantly gestured that we remain seated. "Not IIT style," he proclaimed in a tremulous voice with a vexed overtone. We were quick to catch the message: respecting professors was a tarnish on the snobbish IIT culture. As such, having recently cleared one of the most competitive entrance examinations to secure a seat in IIT, we freshers had bloated egos. For us, being disrespectful was a piece of cake. And that piece of cake got iced that day when the professor's advice whipped up our arrogance. Speaking for myself, that instruction from that elderly man is the only one from my undergrad days that I remember to this day.

So we students never rose for another professor again, until our seventh semester.

In the seventh semester, in a select few courses, we undergraduates were joined by postgraduates who had done their bachelors at other engineering colleges, where students were "prehistoric" and rose from their seats to greet every professor. And even after joining IIT, these postgraduates refused to evolve, stubbornly sticking to their old ways. Whenever professors strutted in, these old-fashioned postgraduates would rise—all heated up—while we undergraduates chilled in our seats, struggling hard to hold back our snickers.

But it was different whenever Professor Goel walked in.

For one thing, Goel was a god of structural engineering. A graduate from IIT, he had completed his postgraduate degree and doctorate at the University of Berkeley, the dream destination for aspiring civil engineers from around the globe. The more we were entranced by his intellect, the more we were convinced—there wasn't a civil engineering problem he hadn't solved, and no question on structures he couldn't answer. Akin to a smart kid playing with Lego, he could toy with beams and columns to design buildings that pierced the skies. In fact, when the Twin World Towers came crashing down on 9/11, some wise postgraduates had wistfully remarked that if only Goel had drawn the blueprints for those buildings, the planes would have bounced off the towers, saving thousands of lives.

Professor Goel's genius accounted for only half his charm. The other half was his disarming disposition. He was ever ready to mentor his students, but never tormented them. He always arrived ahead of time for his lectures and then stood at the door of the classroom, patiently waiting for all the students to arrive. Once when I missed his class, he asked me the reason for my absence when we crossed each other in the corridor. His inquiry had an overtone of concern, not criticism. I was touched, but all the more surprised. How could he make out one missing student in a classroom of 90-odd?

Because he loved his students, he naturally enjoyed teaching. If he were to walk into any of the construction-business MNCs in Mumbai, he would be glad-handed with a top brass job, slam dunk. His CV was impressive for sure; equally mind-blowing was how up to speed he kept himself on the latest developments in his field. And yet, forgoing lucrative prospects, he was content with the relatively lower-paying profession of a teacher, for the sake of his students.

Whenever he walked into the class, even we undergraduates sprang from our seats, unbidden. We chucked away our "IIT style" to offer him the respect he was due.

He had disarmed us emotionally through his charming personality, which was a riveting blend of greatness and sweetness...

... in much the same way as Lord Sri Krishna conquers the heart of a Karma Yogi.

> A Karma Yogi who has realised me through the awakening of Jnana knows me to be the ultimate beneficiary of all yajnas

and austerities mentioned in the Vedas, the Supreme Lord of all planets and demigods, and at the same time, the dearest friend and well-wisher of all living entities. Such a person attains inner peace. (Bhagavad Gita 5.29)

An enlightened person is not attracted to material sense pleasure but is always in a trance, enjoying the pleasure within. In this way, the self-realised person enjoys unlimited happiness by concentrating on the Supreme. (Bhagavad Gita 5.21)

With that higher spiritual experience, being purpose-driven to serve God is natural for a Karma Yogi, and letting go of material identities is easy. Just as for us undergraduates, with Professor Goel entering our lives, relinquishing the identity of being the smart alecs was a breeze.

On the path towards the awakening of Jnana and progress in Karma Yoga, the Yajna that's gaining the most traction in the modern world is *Sankirtana Yajna*. And that's for good reason.

The Charm of Sankirtana Yajna

Sankirtana Yajna, colloquially called *Kirtan*, is the singing of the holy names of God to the accompaniment of music in a call-and-response fashion.

An article in *The Washington Post*, published in 2013, noted the meteoric rise in Kirtan's popularity in the Western World:

> Demand is suddenly so great that kirtans are being offered at many local studios for yoga, which, like meditation, has become a gateway to the transcendent for millions of secular Americans who still, in some quiet corner, believe in God.

The *Post* went on to describe the experience of 40-year-old Beth Swick, a project manager for architecture and design firms in Montgomery County, when she attended Kirtan for the first time:

> ...enveloped by the rich music and the group repetition of a single sacred phrase (although at the time indecipherable to her), Swick felt powerfully connected to something divine.

Swami Prabhupada, the pioneer of the Kirtan revolution in the West who specifically expounded the *Hare Krishna Mahamantra*, had offered an explanation to such experiences way back in 1966:

> This chanting of Hare Krishna, Hare Krishna, Krishna Krishna, Hare Hare/ Hare Rama, Hare Rama, Rama Rama, Hare Hare is directly enacted from the spiritual platform, and thus this sound vibration surpasses all lower strata of consciousness—namely sensual, mental, and intellectual. There is no need, therefore, to understand the language of the mantra, nor is there any need for mental speculation or any intellectual adjustment for chanting this Mahamantra. It springs automatically from the spiritual platform, and as such, anyone can take part in the chanting without any previous qualification...

In essence, the charm of Kirtan lies in its ability to give a direct experience of God even to a first-time participant.

While in the short-run it acts like "beginner's luck", the same Kirtan, or Sankirtana Yajna, if performed regularly, acts along the same line as any other Yajna of the Vedic era. It nurtures in you an attitude of dependency on God, and a desire to selflessly serve Him. These two cardinal principles—selflessness and dependency—that raise your consciousness to Jnana, complete self-realisation, are inherent within the mood and meaning of the Mahamantra. Swami Prabhupada explained the mood in which the Mahamantra is to be sung: "The chanting is a spiritual call for the Lord and His internal energy, Hara, to give protection to the conditioned soul. This chanting is exactly like the genuine cry of a child for its mother. Mother Hara helps the devotee achieve the grace of the Supreme Father, Hari, or Krishna, and the Lord reveals Himself to the devotee who chants this mantra sincerely." As for the meaning of the mantra, it is most commonly translated as "O Lord Krishna, O Lord Rama, O energy of the Lord Hara, please engage me in Your service."

Swami Prabhupada also insisted that Sankirtan Yajna be followed by the distribution of sumptuous prasadam (sanctified food) to all participants, in the same manner as yajna performances were concluded in Vedic culture. That's another aspect that nurtures a selfless attitude, as we previously discussed.

Japa Yajna

Japa Yajna is similar to Sankirtan Yajna in that it is also about chanting God's holy names. The difference is that in *Japa*, there is no musical accompaniment, and the chanter chants softly on prayer beads, often alone. Lord Sri Krishna qualified Japa as the topmost yajna by uttering *yajnaanaam japa yajno 'smi* in the tenth Adhyaaya of the Bhagavad Gita.

Arvind Mafatlal, whom we met in the previous chapter, practised Japa Yajna for one hour in the morning and one hour in the evening. Owing to its simplicity and flexibility, he never had to miss it even when he was travelling abroad or through the rural belt of India. Even in medieval times, the yajna that Chhatrapati Shivaji found most practical was Japa. Sant Tukaram was the guru who initiated him into the process. And for you too, Kirtan and Japa may prove to be the most doable Yajnas on your journey of Karma Yoga.

In Conclusion

On October 7, 1972, approximately six years and six months after Swami Prabhupada lectured at the rundown loft in the Bowery where he criticised Arjuna's peace proposal on the battlefield of Kurukshetra, he was discoursing at a delightful hall at the University of California in Berkeley. Following the talk, snack bags filled with popcorn Prasadam were given out to the attendees. The Swami also had some of the fluffy, spiced kernels and was pleased. "Oh, this is nice," he exclaimed.

The next evening, he had a speaking engagement elsewhere. When it ended, his followers enthusiastically offered him a bag full of popcorn, hoping that the Swami would relish it again. But this time, he refused: "No, I am old. I cannot do things like that very often... it is very difficult for me to digest." He then concluded the issue with a positive note: "It is very good. I like it."

On the way back from the speaking venue, the Swami revealed to his secretary that if he ate something in the evening that was difficult to digest, it would interfere with his rising at 2:00 a.m. to translate Vedic scriptures from Sanskrit to English.

The Swami didn't *want* the popcorn, in the sense that he wasn't hankering for it. Nevertheless, he *liked* it, in that he relished it when someone offered it of their own volition. That he merely relished those snacks—and didn't hanker for them—was demonstrated when he let go of them with ease when they interfered with his purpose.

This quasi-uneventful incident in the life of Swami Prabhupada—who was by then the guru of thousands of Karma Yogis across the globe—demonstrates a fact that's corroborated even by modern science: that "wanting" a thing is different from "liking" it.

In his book *Irresistible*, author Adam Alter cites research by neuroscientist Kent Berridge in which a mischief of rats was given a delicious sugary liquid. After eagerly drinking it, they licked their lips—an indication of the pleasure they had experienced. Next, brain surgery was performed on them to stop dopamine production. Now, when the same group was given the same sweet substance, their eagerness for it was gone. However, when the liquid was fed to them anyway, the rats responded by licking their lips. The conclusion—the surgery had stopped them from "wanting" the delicious sugary syrup, but they continued to "like" it.

The take-home lesson for you from the Swami's story and the experimental findings is this: even as a Karma Yogi, you may accept what your senses *like*. But because of your inner fulfilment, you will be able to relish these external delights with a sense of detachment. You won't be addicted to these pleasures, enabling you to let go of them effortlessly in case they interfere with your purpose.

To conclude, when you are situated in Karma Yoga, you are in the driver's seat relishing life to the fullest—not just through inner fulfilment, but also through external delights—while steering clear of enslavement by the likes and dislikes of the mind and senses.